Hunt's®
Easy Family
Dinners

To Jeff & Sheryl Stratton
From Joanne Kimmel

GREETINGS FROM HUNT'S®

Hunt's *Easy Family Dinners* is sure to become a resource you'll turn to again and again for flavorful meals your family will slow down to enjoy. These recipes feature the convenience and full flavors of Hunt's tomato products in dishes from international favorites to five-ingredient dishes, as well as clever ways to please children from tots to teens.

Beyond packing flavor and ease into your family's meals, tomatoes also fit into a healthful, cancer-fighting diet. An excellent source of vitamin C, and a fat-free food, tomatoes are loaded, too, with the antioxidant lycopene. Research indicates that diets rich in lycopene may reduce a person's risk of developing certain forms of cancer. In fact, a large-scale Harvard University study found that men who ate at least 10 servings of tomato-based foods each week were 45 percent less likely to develop prostrate cancer. Lycopene is what gives tomatoes their rich, red color and, because it remains stable during heating, you can be assured of getting this nutritional benefit with processed tomato products.

You'll find it easy to serve your family meals that are as wholesome as they are great tasting with today's vast variety of Hunt's convenient products and this recipe collection.

Here's to your health—
from Hunt's, the tomato experts!

TABLE OF CONTENTS

Pictured on the cover: Super Chunky Pasta Sauce (see recipe, page 45).

This seal assures you that every recipe in *Hunt's® Easy Family Dinners*
has been tested in the *Better Homes and Gardens®* Test Kitchen.
This means that each recipe is practical and reliable, and meets high
standards of taste appeal.

© Copyright 1996 Meredith Corporation. All rights reserved.
Produced by Meredith Custom Publishing, 1912 Grand Ave., Des Moines, Iowa 50309-3379.
Canadian BN 12348 2887 RT. Printed in the U.S.A.

Hunts®, Homestyle™, Choice-Cut™, Wesson®, La Choy®, Knott's®, Healthy Choice®, and Orville
Redenbacher's® Gourmet® are registered trademarks of Hunt-Wesson, Inc.

THE TREASURE IN THE PANTRY

What a find! Look no further than Hunt's® tomato products when searching for creative dinner ideas. Robust tomato flavors, rich textures, and savory seasonings make a meal in minutes.

FAST FABULOUS FARE

Forget about measuring, chopping, or blending! Save time and energy with Hunt's Ready Tomato Sauces, designed to cut your preparation time. Use your imagination with nine different varieties of rich, thick tomato sauce and tasty herbs and spices. Seven chunky and four smooth sauces boast all-natural ingredients and delicate seasonings ideal for meat, pasta, poultry, and fish.

YOUR CHOICE FOR QUALITY

For any recipe that calls for tomatoes, keep Hunt's Choice-Cut™ Diced Tomatoes on hand. They are the perfect blend of texture and taste. These vine-ripened California tomatoes are picked at the peak of the season, then peeled and diced for optimal flavor—an easy alternative to whole, fresh tomatoes. For extra convenience, try flavorful Choice-Cut Diced Tomatoes with Italian-Style Herbs and Choice-Cut Diced Tomatoes with Roasted Garlic.

BURSTING WITH FLAVOR

Hunt's Tomato Paste thickens your favorite spaghetti or pizza sauces, and adds substance to chili, soups, and stews. The tomato taste has just the right zip in both original and no-salt-added varieties.

Hunt's Tomato Sauce is the perfect consistency for slow-cooking casseroles, soups, and one-dish entrées. Made from highest-quality, rich red tomatoes pureed for a wonderfully thick tomato taste, Hunt's Tomato Sauce is a must in any kitchen. Available in original or no-salt-added varieties.

NATURALLY SATISFYING

The plump red tomatoes in Hunt's Whole Tomatoes and Stewed Tomatoes are remarkably versatile. Both products take the best of California's crop to give you an ingredient that's essential to so many well-liked dishes. Use Whole Tomatoes for a rich tomato taste, or try Hunt's Stewed Tomatoes with a blend of onions, sweet peppers, and celery. Original or no-salt-added versions enhance soups, sauces, and stews.

FOR PASTA LOVERS

Savor the flavors of Hunt's premium-quality Spaghetti Sauces in 14 appetizing blends. With 100% natural ingredients, all varieties are simmered slowly with herbs and spices to create quick sensations that rival homemade sauces.

Just heat and serve over any kind of pasta or noodle, and Hunt's Spaghetti Sauces will become your family's favorites — not only for their perfectly simmered flavor, but for outstanding value and convenience, too. Choose from Hunt's Original, Homestyle™ (no sugar added), Classic Garlic and Herb, Chunky (with lots of peeled, diced tomatoes), and Light varieties to bring tantalizing options to your table.

5-INGREDIENT DISHES

• • • • • • • •

When do just five simple ingredients add up to full-flavored dishes? When you have Hunt's® Ready Tomato Sauces at your fingertips to replace a multitude of ingredients. You'll save time yet still add home-cooked taste your family will love. When you call on Colorful Italian Sausage and Peppers, Time-Saver Chicken, and the other quick dishes in this chapter, you'll be enjoying great tasting meals in no time at all.

Colorful Italian Sausage and Peppers (see recipe, page 8)

COLORFUL ITALIAN SAUSAGE AND PEPPERS

MAKES 4 SERVINGS
TOTAL TIME: 25 MINUTES

1 pound fresh Italian sausage links, cooked*
1 medium onion, sliced
1 tablespoon Wesson® Oil

3 sweet peppers (red, yellow, and/or green), cut into ½-inch-thick slices
1 15-ounce can Hunt's® Ready Tomato Sauces Chunky Italian

Cut sausage into 2-inch slices. In skillet cook onion in hot Wesson Oil over medium heat 2 minutes. Add peppers and cook 4 to 5 minutes more or until crisp-tender; drain. Stir sausage and Hunt's Ready Tomato Sauces Chunky Italian into vegetables; cook until heated through.

*Note: To cook sausage, prick each link 2 or 3 times with fork. In 12-inch skillet cook sausage over medium heat 2 to 3 minutes or until brown. Remove from heat. Carefully add ½ cup water to skillet. Bring to boiling; reduce heat. Simmer, covered, 10 to 12 minutes or until cooked through and juices run clear. Remove; drain on paper towels.

Nutrition facts per serving: 374 cal., 19 g pro., 15 g carbo., 27 g total fat (8 g sat. fat), 65 mg chol., 3 g dietary fiber, 1,260 mg sodium. Daily Value: 48% vit. A, 163% vit. C, 14% iron.

Give It a Garlic Boost

If you and your family like garlic, it's easy to tailor the recipe above to suit your tastes. Just choose a spicy sausage and use Hunt's® Ready Tomato Sauces Chunky Garlic and Herb instead of Hunt's Ready Tomato Sauces Chunky Italian. The mellow garlic flavor will complement the onion and sweet peppers in this savory dish.

Sizzlin' Sweet Ribs

MAKES 4 SERVINGS
PREPARATION TIME: 10 MINUTES • COOKING TIME: 1¼ HOURS

1 15-ounce can Hunt's® Ready Tomato Sauces Chunky Salsa	1 teaspoon garlic salt
½ to ¾ cup packed brown sugar	3 pounds baby back (pork loin back) ribs
¼ cup orange juice	

In bowl combine Hunt's Ready Tomato Sauces Chunky Salsa, brown sugar, orange juice, and garlic salt. Lightly brush on both sides of ribs. Place ribs, bone-side down, on rack in roasting pan. Bake, covered, in 400° oven 45 minutes. Pour remaining salsa mixture over ribs. Bake, uncovered, 30 minutes more or until tender. To serve, spoon juices over ribs.

Nutrition facts per serving: 423 cal., 23 g pro., 32 g carbo., 23 g total fat (9 g sat. fat), 89 mg chol., 2 g dietary fiber, 1,139 mg sodium. Daily Value: 1% vit. A, 56% vit. C, 19% iron.

Noodle Supper in No Time

MAKES 4 OR 5 SERVINGS
TOTAL TIME: 20 MINUTES

1 pound ground beef	1 15-ounce can whole kernel corn
1 medium onion, chopped (½ cup)	2 3-ounce packages Oriental noodles with beef flavor
1 15-ounce can Hunt's® Ready Tomato Sauces Chunky Tomato	

In 12-inch skillet cook ground beef and onion until meat is brown; drain. Stir in Hunt's Ready Tomato Sauces Chunky Tomato, *undrained* corn, and seasonings from 1 package of noodles (reserve remaining seasoning to use as soup flavoring). Stir in ½ cup *water*.

Break up noodles from both packages; add to skillet. Bring to boiling; reduce heat. Simmer, covered, 8 to 10 minutes or until noodles are tender.

Nutrition facts per serving: 499 cal., 29 g pro., 45 g carbo., 23 g total fat (6 g sat. fat), 71 mg chol., 3 g dietary fiber, 1,877 mg sodium. Daily Value: 11% vit. A, 37% vit. C, 24% iron.

ITALIAN MEATBALLS

MAKES 6 SERVINGS
PREPARATION TIME: 15 MINUTES • COOKING TIME: 15 MINUTES

1½ pounds lean ground beef
½ cup fine dry seasoned bread crumbs
2 slightly beaten eggs

2 15-ounce cans Hunt's® Ready Tomato Sauces Chunky Garlic and Herb
1 tablespoon cornstarch

In bowl combine beef, bread crumbs, eggs, and ¼ teaspoon *pepper*. Shape into thirty-six 1½-inch balls; place in 15x10x1-inch baking pan. Bake, uncovered, in 375° oven 15 to 20 minutes or until no longer pink in center; drain.

Meanwhile, in saucepan combine Hunt's Ready Tomato Sauces Chunky Garlic and Herb and cornstarch. Cook and stir until thickened and bubbly. Cook and stir 2 minutes more. Gently stir in meatballs; heat through. If desired, serve over hot cooked pasta.

Nutrition facts per serving: 323 cal., 26 g pro., 24 g carbo., 14 g total fat (5 g sat. fat), 142 mg chol., 2 g dietary fiber, 748 mg sodium. Daily Value: 7% vit. A, 53% vit. C, 25% iron.

Italian Meatballs

Fiesta Minute Steaks

Makes 4 Servings
Preparation Time: 10 Minutes • Cooking Time: 22 Minutes

- 4   ¼-pound beef cubed steaks
- 1   tablespoon Wesson® Oil
- 1   15-ounce can Hunt's® Ready Tomato Sauces Chunky Salsa
- 6   cups shredded lettuce
- 1   cup finely shredded cheddar cheese (4 ounces)

In skillet cook steaks in hot Wesson Oil over medium heat until brown, turning once. Add Hunt's Ready Tomato Sauces Chunky Salsa. Bring to boiling; reduce heat. Simmer, covered, 15 minutes or until steaks are tender. Serve steaks on lettuce. Top with sauce and cheese.

Nutrition facts per serving: 359 cal., 37 g pro., 11 g carbo., 19 g total fat (8 g sat. fat), 102 mg chol., 2 g dietary fiber, 787 mg sodium. Daily Value: 12% vit. A, 49% vit. C, 26% iron.

Salsa-Special Chicken

Makes 4 Servings
Preparation Time: 10 Minutes • Cooking Time: 30 Minutes

- 4   medium skinless, boneless chicken breast halves
- 1   15-ounce can Hunt's® Ready Tomato Sauces Chunky Salsa
- 6   cups purchased torn mixed salad greens
- ¼   cup sliced green onions
- ½   cup frozen avocado dip, thawed

Place chicken on unheated rack of broiler pan. Broil 4 to 5 inches from heat 7 minutes. Turn and broil 5 to 8 minutes more or until tender and no longer pink, brushing with some of the Hunt's Ready Tomato Sauces Chunky Salsa. In saucepan heat remaining sauce. Arrange chicken on salad greens; sprinkle with green onions. Serve with avocado dip and remaining sauce.

Nutrition facts per serving: 224 cal., 25 g pro., 14 g carbo., 8 g total fat (1 g sat. fat), 59 mg chol., 3 g dietary fiber, 828 mg sodium. Daily Value: 16% vit. A, 66% vit. C, 17% iron.

TIME-SAVER CHICKEN

MAKES 4 SERVINGS
PREPARATION TIME: 5 MINUTES • COOKING TIME: 50 MINUTES

4 small chicken breast halves, skinned
½ teaspoon garlic salt

Dash pepper
1 15-ounce can Hunt's® Ready Tomato Sauces Chunky Special

Sprinkle chicken with garlic salt and pepper. Place chicken in lightly greased 3-quart rectangular baking dish. Pour Hunt's Ready Tomato Sauces Chunky Special over chicken. Bake, covered, in 350° oven 50 to 55 minutes or until chicken is tender and no longer pink. To serve, spoon tomato sauce over chicken. If desired, serve with hot cooked rice.

Nutrition facts per serving: 188 cal., 23 g pro., 13 g carbo., 5 g total fat (1 g sat. fat), 59 mg chol., 2 g dietary fiber, 775 mg sodium. Daily Value: 20% vit. A, 26% vit. C, 4% iron.

BREADED CHICKEN WITH GREEN BEANS

MAKES 4 SERVINGS
PREPARATION TIME: 10 MINUTES • COOKING TIME: 16 MINUTES

¼ cup all-purpose flour
4 medium skinless, boneless chicken breast halves
2 tablespoons Wesson® Oil

2 cups loose-pack frozen French-style green beans
1 15-ounce can Hunt's® Ready Tomato Sauces Chunky Italian

In shallow bowl stir together flour, ½ teaspoon *salt*, and ¼ teaspoon *pepper*. Dip chicken in flour mixture to coat. In skillet cook chicken in hot Wesson Oil over medium-high heat 8 to 10 minutes or until tender and no longer pink, turning once. Remove chicken; cover and keep warm.

In same skillet combine beans and Hunt's Ready Tomato Sauces Chunky Italian. Bring to boiling; reduce heat. Simmer, covered, 5 minutes. Return chicken to skillet. Cover and cook 1 to 2 minutes more or until heated through.

Nutrition facts per serving: 276 cal., 25 g pro., 17 g carbo., 12 g total fat (2 g sat. fat), 59 mg chol., 2 g dietary fiber, 824 mg sodium. Daily Value: 11% vit. A, 13% vit. C, 15% iron.

ROMAN HOLIDAY CHICKEN AND FETTUCCINE

MAKES 3 SERVINGS
TOTAL TIME: 20 MINUTES

2 cups frozen pepper stir-fry vegetables (yellow, green, and red peppers and onion)
1 15-ounce can Hunt's® Ready Tomato Sauces Chunky Italian
1 cup cubed cooked chicken

6 ounces packaged dried fettuccine, cooked and drained
2 tablespoons grated Parmesan cheese

In saucepan stir together vegetables, Hunt's Ready Tomato Sauces Chunky Italian, and chicken; bring to boiling. Season to taste with black pepper. Spoon over fettuccine. Toss to coat. Sprinkle with Parmesan cheese.

Nutrition facts per serving: 439 cal., 27 g pro., 62 g carbo., 9 g total fat (2 g sat. fat), 48 mg chol., 3 g dietary fiber, 800 mg sodium. Daily Value: 73% vit. A, 48% vit. C, 24% iron.

TAKE-IT-EASY CHEESE CAVATELLI

MAKES 6 SERVINGS
PREPARATION TIME: 25 MINUTES • COOKING TIME: 30 MINUTES

1 27-ounce can Hunt's® Original Spaghetti Sauce Traditional
10 ounces packaged dried cavatelli, cooked and drained

6 ounces provolone cheese, sliced
2 tablespoons grated Parmesan cheese

Spread ¼ *cup* Hunt's Original Spaghetti Sauce Traditional in 2-quart rectangular baking dish. Top with *half* of the cavatelli, *half* of the provolone cheese, and *half* of the remaining spaghetti sauce. Repeat layers.

Bake, covered, in 350° oven 20 minutes. Sprinkle with Parmesan cheese. Bake, uncovered, 10 minutes more or until heated through.

Nutrition facts per serving: 392 cal., 18 g pro., 56 g carbo., 13 g total fat (5 g sat. fat), 22 mg chol., 7 g dietary fiber, 1,328 mg sodium. Daily Value: 17% vit. A, 33% vit. C, 26% iron.

TORTELLINI WITH ROSEMARY TOMATO SAUCE

MAKES 3 SERVINGS
TOTAL TIME: 17 MINUTES

1 **15-ounce can Hunt's® Ready Tomato Sauces Chunky Italian**	½ **teaspoon finely shredded lemon peel**
1 **teaspoon snipped fresh rosemary or ¼ teaspoon dried rosemary, crushed**	1 **9-ounce package refrigerated or frozen cheese- or meat-filled tortellini, cooked and drained**
¼ **cup sliced pitted ripe olives or one 2½-ounce jar sliced mushrooms**	

In saucepan mix Hunt's Ready Tomato Sauces Chunky Italian and rosemary. Bring to boiling; reduce heat. Simmer, uncovered, 4 minutes. Stir in olives, lemon peel, and enough water to make of desired consistency. Heat through. Spoon over tortellini.

Nutrition facts per serving: 342 cal., 15 g pro., 49 g carbo., 10 g total fat (2 g sat. fat), 40 mg chol., 3 g dietary fiber, 1,021 mg sodium. Daily Value: 11% vit. A, 5% vit. C, 18% iron.

PASTA WITH SHRIMP SAUCE

MAKES 4 SERVINGS
TOTAL TIME: 25 MINUTES

¾ **pound peeled and deveined fresh or frozen shrimp or 1½ cups cubed cooked chicken**	1 **6-ounce can Hunt's® Tomato Paste**
2 **14½-ounce cans Hunt's® Choice-Cut™ Diced Tomatoes with Italian Style Herbs**	1 **2¼-ounce can sliced pitted ripe olives**
	½ **pound packaged dried mostaccioli or rigatoni, cooked and drained**

Thaw shrimp, if frozen; drain. In saucepan combine Hunt's Choice-Cut Diced Tomatoes with Italian Style Herbs, Hunt's Tomato Paste, and olives. Bring to boiling. Add shrimp. Return to boiling; reduce heat. Simmer, uncovered, 3 minutes or until shrimp turn pink, stirring occasionally. Add cooked mostaccioli; toss gently to coat.

Nutrition facts per serving: 400 cal., 25 g pro., 63 g carbo., 6 g total fat (1 g sat. fat), 131 mg chol., 4 g dietary fiber, 1,390 mg sodium. Daily Value: 34% vit. A, 87% vit. C, 40% iron.

South-of-the-Border Broiled Fish

MAKES 4 SERVINGS
PREPARATION TIME: 5 MINUTES • COOKING TIME: 4 MINUTES

- 1 **pound fresh or frozen red snapper fillets, ½ inch thick**
- 1 **tablespoon butter or margarine, melted**
- ¼ to ½ **teaspoon chili powder**

- 1 **15-ounce can Hunt's® Ready Tomato Sauces Chunky Salsa**
- 1 **8-ounce can crushed pineapple (juice pack), drained**

Thaw fish, if frozen. Cut fish into serving-size portions. Combine butter and chili powder; brush on both sides of fish. Place fish on unheated rack of broiler pan. Broil 4 inches from heat 4 to 6 minutes or until fish flakes easily with a fork, turning once.

Meanwhile, in saucepan combine Hunt's Ready Tomato Sauces Chunky Salsa and pineapple; heat through. Spoon over broiled fish.

Nutrition facts per serving: 216 cal., 25 g pro., 19 g carbo., 5 g total fat (2 g sat. fat), 49 mg chol., 2 g dietary fiber, 633 mg sodium. Daily Value: 4% vit. A, 53% vit. C, 9% iron.

Fish Napoli

MAKES 4 SERVINGS
PREPARATION TIME: 5 MINUTES • COOKING TIME: 20 MINUTES

- 8 **2-ounce frozen, crumb-coated, batter-fried fish fillets**
- 1 **14½-ounce can Hunt's® Choice-Cut™ Diced Tomatoes with Italian Style Herbs**

- 1 **4½-ounce jar sliced mushrooms, drained**
- 1 **tablespoon cornstarch**
- 2 **tablespoons grated Parmesan cheese**

Bake frozen fish according to package directions. Meanwhile, in saucepan combine Hunt's Choice-Cut Diced Tomatoes with Italian Style Herbs, mushrooms, cornstarch, and ⅛ to ¼ teaspoon *pepper*. Cook and stir until thickened and bubbly. Cook and stir 2 minutes more. Remove from heat. Spoon tomato mixture over fish. Sprinkle with Parmesan cheese.

Nutrition facts per serving: 325 cal., 37 g pro., 17 g carbo., 11 g total fat (3 g sat. fat), 86 mg chol., 2 g dietary fiber, 948 mg sodium. Daily Value: 7% vit. A, 30% vit. C, 15% iron.

SEAFOOD-ARTICHOKE PIZZAS

MAKES 8 SERVINGS
PREPARATION TIME: 15 MINUTES • COOKING TIME: 15 MINUTES

1   8- or 9-ounce package frozen
    artichoke hearts or one 6-ounce
    jar sliced mushrooms, drained
2   10-ounce packages refrigerated
    pizza dough
1   15-ounce can Hunt's® Ready
    Tomato Sauces Original Italian

2   6-ounce packages frozen, peeled,
    cooked shrimp, thawed, or two
    8-ounce packages crab-flavored
    salad-style fish
½   cup grated Parmesan cheese

Cook artichoke hearts according to package directions. Drain; cool slightly. Cut into bite-size pieces.

Unroll pizza dough and transfer to 2 lightly greased 11- to 13-inch pizza pans. Press dough out and build up edges slightly. Prick generously with fork. Bake in 425° oven 10 minutes or until light brown.

Spread Hunt's Ready Tomato Sauces Original Italian over hot crusts. Arrange artichoke hearts and shrimp over sauce. Sprinkle with Parmesan cheese. Bake 5 to 7 minutes more or until heated through.

Nutrition facts per serving: 277 cal., 19 g pro., 38 g carbo., 6 g total fat (2 g sat. fat), 88 mg chol., 2 g dietary fiber, 695 mg sodium. Daily Value: 13% vit. A, 15% vit. C, 26% iron.

Pizza Pizzazz

Create a mouthwatering pizza in no time with Hunt's® Ready Tomato Sauces and a few ingredients. Team Hunt's Ready Tomato Sauces Chunky or Original Italian with pepperoni, onion, sweet pepper, and mozzarella cheese. Use Hunt's Ready Tomato Sauces Chunky Chili with sausage, mushrooms, and Monterey Jack cheese. Try Hunt's Ready Tomato Sauces Chunky Salsa with ground beef or ham, green onion, and cheddar or colby cheese. Or, start with your favorite flavor of Hunt's Ready Tomato Sauces and create your own one-of-a-kind combo.

TOMATO TABBOULEH

MAKES 8 SIDE-DISH SERVINGS
PREPARATION TIME: 10 MINUTES • CHILLING TIME: 8 HOURS

1 cup bulgur	1 large cucumber, coarsely chopped
1 15-ounce can Hunt's® Ready Tomato Sauces Chunky Garlic and Herb	½ cup finely chopped green onion
	½ cup snipped fresh parsley

Place bulgur in colander. Rinse with cold water; drain well. In bowl combine drained bulgur, Hunt's Ready Tomato Sauces Chunky Garlic and Herb, cucumber, and onion. Cover and refrigerate 8 to 24 hours. Before serving, stir parsley into bulgur mixture.

Nutrition facts per serving: 92 cal., 3 g pro., 20 g carbo., 1 g total fat (0 g sat. fat), 0 mg chol., 5 g dietary fiber, 169 mg sodium. Daily Value: 5% vit. A, 31% vit. C, 8% iron.

ZUCCHINI PASTA TOSS

MAKES 6 SIDE-DISH SERVINGS
TOTAL TIME: 25 MINUTES

¼ pound packaged dried medium bow-tie pasta	1 15-ounce can Hunt's® Ready Tomato Sauces Chunky Special
3 medium zucchini, thinly sliced	½ teaspoon dried thyme or basil, crushed

Cook pasta according to package directions, adding zucchini for last 2 minutes of cooking. Drain well. Meanwhile, in saucepan combine Hunt's Ready Tomato Sauces Chunky Special and thyme; heat through. Toss with pasta mixture.

Nutrition facts per serving: 124 cal., 4 g pro., 25 g carbo., 1 g total fat (0 g sat. fat), 0 mg chol., 2 g dietary fiber, 312 mg sodium. Daily Value: 14% vit. A, 21% vit. C, 5% iron.

EASY EGGPLANT PARMIGIANA

MAKES 4 SIDE-DISH SERVINGS
PREPARATION TIME: 10 MINUTES • COOKING TIME: 6 MINUTES

1 small eggplant (about 12 ounces)	1 cup shredded mozzarella cheese (4 ounces)
1 tablespoon Wesson® Oil	
1 15-ounce can Hunt's® Ready Tomato Sauces Chunky Italian	2 tablespoons grated Parmesan or Romano cheese

Peel eggplant, if desired. Slice crosswise into ½-inch-thick slices. Brush lightly with Wesson Oil. Place eggplant on unheated rack of broiler pan. Broil 3 to 4 inches from heat 6 to 8 minutes or until tender, turning once.

Meanwhile, in saucepan heat Hunt's Ready Tomato Sauces Chunky Italian until bubbly. Place eggplant on platter; spoon sauce over. Sprinkle with mozzarella and Parmesan cheeses.

Nutrition facts per serving: 186 cal., 10 g pro., 13 g carbo., 11 g total fat (4 g sat. fat), 18 mg chol., 4 g dietary fiber, 687 mg sodium. Daily Value: 13% vit. A, 4% vit. C, 6% iron.

Tomato Tabbouleh,
Easy Eggplant Parmigiana

KID PLEASIN' MEALS

Frowns turn into happy smiles when French Bread Pizza is on the menu. Flavor-packed Hunt's® tomato products make mealtime fun and get your family to the table fast. Even persnickety preschoolers and junk-food-loving teens will look forward to dinner at home when A+ Turkey Lasagna and Tip-Top Tortilla Roll-Ups are mealtime stars.

French Bread Pizza
(see recipe, page 22)

FRENCH BREAD PIZZA

MAKES 4 TO 6 SERVINGS
PREPARATION TIME: 10 MINUTES • COOKING TIME: 10 MINUTES

1 loaf unsliced French bread, sliced in half horizontally
2 tablespoons Wesson® Oil
1 15-ounce can Hunt's® Ready Tomato Sauces Chunky Italian
1 cup shredded mozzarella cheese (4 ounces)
1 cup shredded Monterey Jack cheese (4 ounces)
2 tablespoons grated Parmesan cheese

Favorite meat topping (such as ½ of a 3½-ounce package sliced pepperoni or 8 ounces cooked and drained ground beef or cubed fully-cooked ham)
Favorite vegetable toppings (such as ½ cup sliced mushrooms, chopped green or yellow sweet pepper, and/or sliced pitted olives)

Place bread, cut sides up, on a large baking sheet. Brush with Wesson Oil. Spoon Hunt's Ready Tomato Sauces Chunky Italian over bread.

In bowl combine mozzarella, Monterey Jack, and Parmesan cheeses. Sprinkle cheese mixture over bread. Top with desired meat and vegetable toppings.

Bake in 425° oven 10 to 15 minutes or until cheeses are melted and bubbly.

Nutrition facts per serving: 678 cal., 29 g pro., 68 g carbo., 32 g total fat (13 g sat. fat), 44 mg chol., 2 g dietary fiber, 1,778 mg sodium. Daily Value: 20% vit. A, 3% vit. C, 27% iron.

Kid-Pleasing Potato Bar

For an easy (and fun!) meal that the children will love, start with hot baked potatoes. Heat one of your favorite Hunt's® Ready Tomato Sauces and set it out with the toppings your children like best, such as shredded cheese, cooked peas or broccoli, shredded lettuce, cubed ham, cooked crumbled bacon, or cooked ground beef. Then, let the kids spoon on some sauce and mix and match their own potato toppings.

FOOT-LONG CHILI DOGS

MAKES 8 SERVINGS
PREPARATION TIME: 10 MINUTES • COOKING TIME: 10 MINUTES

1   pound ground beef
1   15-ounce can Hunt's® Ready
    Tomato Sauces Chunky Chili
1   15-ounce can red kidney beans,
    drained

8   foot-long or extra-long
    frankfurters, cooked
8   foot-long or regular frankfurter
    buns

In skillet cook beef until brown; drain. Stir in Hunt's Ready Tomato Sauces Chunky Chili and beans. Bring to boiling; reduce heat. Simmer, uncovered, 5 minutes; stir occasionally. Place frankfurters in buns; top with meat mixture. If desired, serve with chopped red onion and shredded cheese.

Nutrition facts per serving: 647 cal., 31 g pro., 51 g carbo., 35 g total fat (14 g sat. fat), 87 mg chol., 5 g dietary fiber, 1,617 mg sodium. Daily Value: 8% vit. A, 38% vit. C, 32% iron.

PIZZA LOVER'S STEW

MAKES 6 SERVINGS
PREPARATION TIME: 15 MINUTES • COOKING TIME: 20 MINUTES

¾   pound bulk pork sausage or
    ground beef
1   cup sliced fresh mushrooms
1   medium onion, chopped (½ cup)
1   28-ounce can Hunt's® Whole
    Tomatoes, cut up

2   cups loose-pack frozen broccoli,
     cauliflower, and carrots
1   15-ounce can Hunt's® Ready
     Tomato Sauces Original Italian
1½ cups Hunt's® Tomato Juice
½   teaspoon fennel seed, crushed
¼   cup grated Parmesan cheese

In large saucepan cook sausage, mushrooms, and onion until meat is brown; drain. Stir in *undrained* Hunt's Whole Tomatoes (cut up), frozen vegetables, Hunt's Ready Tomato Sauces Original Italian, Hunt's Tomato Juice, and fennel seed. Bring to boiling; reduce heat. Simmer, covered, 15 minutes. Sprinkle each serving with Parmesan cheese.

Nutrition facts per serving: 206 cal., 11 g pro., 20 g carbo., 10 g total fat (4 g sat. fat), 26 mg chol., 5 g dietary fiber, 1,152 mg sodium. Daily Value: 82% vit. A, 91% vit. C, 17% iron.

AWESOME BARBECUED RIBS

MAKES 4 SERVINGS
PREPARATION TIME: 5 MINUTES • COOKING TIME: 1½ HOURS

2½ to 3 pounds baby back (pork loin back) ribs or pork spareribs, cut into 2-rib pieces
1 medium onion, chopped (½ cup)
½ teaspoon minced garlic (1 clove)
1 tablespoon Wesson® Oil
1 8-ounce can Hunt's® Tomato Sauce

⅓ cup Knott's® Orange Marmalade
2 tablespoons frozen orange juice concentrate, thawed
1 tablespoon La Choy® Soy Sauce
1 tablespoon lemon juice
½ teaspoon ground ginger
¼ teaspoon ground allspice

Place ribs, bone side down, on rack in roasting pan. Roast, uncovered, in 350° oven 1 hour; drain.

Meanwhile, for sauce, in saucepan cook onion and garlic in hot Wesson Oil until onion is tender. Stir in Hunt's Tomato Sauce, Knott's Orange Marmalade, orange juice concentrate, La Choy Soy Sauce, lemon juice, ginger, and allspice. Bring to boiling; reduce heat. Simmer, uncovered, 15 minutes, stirring occasionally.

Spoon some of the sauce over ribs. Roast ribs, covered, 30 to 45 minutes more or until tender, occasionally spooning sauce over ribs. Before serving, brush ribs with any remaining sauce.

Nutrition facts per serving: 436 cal., 23 g pro., 29 g carbo., 26 g total fat (9 g sat. fat), 89 mg chol., 3 g dietary fiber, 686 mg sodium. Daily Value: 6% vit. A, 44% vit. C, 15% iron.

CELEBRATION PORK CHOPS

MAKES 4 SERVINGS
PREPARATION TIME: 25 MINUTES • COOKING TIME: 40 MINUTES

1 **pound sweet potatoes, peeled and cut into 1-inch chunks**	1 **14½-ounce can Hunt's® Choice-Cut™ Diced Tomatoes**
4 **pork loin chops, cut ¾ inch thick (about 1½ pounds total)**	1 **8-ounce can pineapple chunks (juice pack)**
1 **tablespoon Wesson® Oil**	½ **teaspoon salt**
1 **medium onion, cut into wedges**	½ **teaspoon ground cinnamon**
1 **medium red sweet pepper, cut into thin strips**	⅛ **teaspoon black pepper**
½ **to 1 teaspoon minced garlic (1 to 2 cloves)**	2 **tablespoons cornstarch**
	1 **tablespoon cold water**
	Hot cooked rice (optional)

In covered saucepan cook potatoes in boiling water 10 to 15 minutes or just until tender; drain. Meanwhile, in skillet cook chops in hot Wesson Oil over medium heat 10 minutes or until brown, turning once. Remove chops from skillet.

In pan drippings cook onion, sweet pepper, and garlic 3 minutes. Stir in *undrained* Hunt's Choice-Cut Diced Tomatoes, *undrained* pineapple, salt, cinnamon, and black pepper. Return chops to skillet. Bring to boiling; reduce heat. Simmer, covered, 30 to 40 minutes or until chops are tender and no longer pink. Remove chops from skillet; cover and keep warm.

Stir together cornstarch and water; add to mixture in skillet. Cook and stir until thickened and bubbly. Cook and stir 2 minutes more. Carefully stir in potatoes; heat through. Serve over chops. If desired, serve with rice.

Nutrition facts per serving: 294 cal., 14 g pro., 42 g carbo., 9 g total fat (2 g sat. fat), 34 mg chol., 5 g dietary fiber, 492 mg sodium. Daily Value: 213% vit. A, 124% vit. C, 8% iron.

Meat Loaf Olé

MAKES 6 TO 8 SERVINGS
PREPARATION TIME: 20 MINUTES • COOKING TIME: 1¼ HOURS

1   15-ounce can Hunt's® Tomato
    Sauce
2   to 3 teaspoons chili powder
¼   teaspoon ground cumin
⅛   teaspoon garlic powder
2   slightly beaten eggs
1   cup finely crushed corn chips
    (3½ ounces)

½   of an 11-ounce can (about ⅔ cup)
    whole kernel corn with sweet
    peppers, drained
1   medium onion, chopped (½ cup)
½   cup sliced stuffed green olives
1   4½-ounce can diced green chili
    peppers, drained
2   pounds lean ground beef

In bowl combine Hunt's Tomato Sauce, chili powder, cumin, and garlic powder. Set aside *half* of the mixture. In bowl combine remaining sauce mixture, eggs, corn chips, corn, onion, olives, and chili peppers. Add ground beef; mix well.

In large shallow baking pan pat meat mixture into 10x5-inch loaf. Bake in 375° oven 70 minutes or until juices run clear, drain. Spoon reserved sauce mixture over loaf; bake 5 minutes more. Transfer meat loaf to platter. Let stand 10 minutes before slicing.

Nutrition facts per serving: 424 cal., 32 g pro., 22 g carbo., 23 g total fat (7 g sat. fat), 166 mg chol., 4 g dietary fiber, 1,013 mg sodium. Daily Value: 15% vit. A, 35% vit. C, 30% iron.

Masterful Meat Loaf

For an even-textured meat loaf, gently mix the ground meat with the other ingredients. Handling the mixture too much causes the meat loaf to become compact. For best results, use your hands instead of a spoon to thoroughly combine the ingredients.

THE ULTIMATE CALZONES

MAKES 6 SERVINGS
PREPARATION TIME: 35 MINUTES • COOKING TIME: 12 MINUTES

½ pound ground beef or pork
1 medium onion, chopped (½ cup)
1 14½-ounce can Hunt's® Choice-
Cut™ Diced Tomatoes with
Italian Style Herbs
¾ cup chopped broccoli
¼ teaspoon pepper
¼ cup sliced pitted ripe olives

2 10-ounce packages refrigerated
pizza dough
1 cup shredded cheddar cheese
(4 ounces)
2 teaspoons milk
¼ cup grated Parmesan cheese
Hunt's® Ready Tomato Sauces
Original Italian (optional)

For filling, in skillet cook beef and onion until meat is brown; drain. Stir in *undrained* Hunt's Choice-Cut Diced Tomatoes with Italian Style Herbs, broccoli, and pepper. Bring to boiling; reduce heat. Simmer, uncovered, 10 minutes or until most of liquid has evaporated, stirring occasionally. Remove from heat. Stir in olives.

Unroll 1 package of pizza dough. On lightly floured surface, roll dough into 15x10-inch rectangle; cut into six 5-inch squares. Repeat with remaining pizza dough. Divide filling among the 12 squares. Sprinkle with cheddar cheese. Fold dough over filling. Using fork, press edges well to seal.

Arrange in 2 greased 15x10x1-inch baking pans. Prick with fork. Brush with milk; sprinkle with Parmesan cheese. Bake in 425° oven 12 to 15 minutes or until golden. If desired, heat Hunt's Ready Tomato Sauces Original Italian and serve with calzones.

Note: If desired, place any leftover calzones in freezer bag, seal, and freeze. To reheat, unwrap and place frozen calzones on baking sheet. Bake in 350° oven 12 to 15 minutes or until heated through.

Nutrition facts per serving: 398 cal., 21 g pro., 41 g carbo., 17 g total fat (7 g sat. fat), 47 mg chol., 3 g dietary fiber, 890 mg sodium. Daily Value: 14% vit. A, 43% vit. C, 22% iron.

The Ultimate Calzones

SUNDAY-NIGHT BURGERS

MAKES 6 SERVINGS
PREPARATION TIME: 10 MINUTES • COOKING TIME: 15 MINUTES

1 pound lean ground beef	Dash salt (optional)
1 medium onion, chopped (½ cup)	1 cup chopped lettuce
1 15-ounce can Hunt's® Ready Tomato Sauces Original Italian	6 hamburger buns, split and toasted
⅓ cup bulgur	¾ cup shredded cheddar cheese (3 ounces)

In skillet cook beef and onion until meat is brown; drain. Stir in Hunt's Ready Tomato Sauces Original Italian, bulgur, and, if desired, salt. Bring to boiling; reduce heat. Simmer, uncovered, 10 minutes or until desired consistency, stirring occasionally. Place lettuce on buns; spoon meat mixture over each. Sprinkle with cheese. Cover with bun tops.

Nutrition facts per serving: 361 cal., 23 g pro., 35 g carbo., 15 g total fat (6 g sat. fat), 63 mg chol., 5 g dietary fiber, 604 mg sodium. Daily Value: 15% vit. A, 10% vit. C, 21% iron.

Bulgur Basics

Bulgur is a wonderful whole-grain product that's packed with protein, minerals, and fiber. It gives foods texture and bulk without adding fat. You'll find it in the rice or cereal sections at most supermarkets.

To store bulgur, place it in an airtight container. Then, store it in a cool, dry place for up to 6 months or in the freezer for up to 2 years.

TACO PIZZAS

MAKES 8 SERVINGS
PREPARATION TIME: 30 MINUTES • COOKING TIME: 7 MINUTES

Cornmeal Pizza Dough (see recipe below) or two 10-ounce packages refrigerated pizza dough
½ pound lean ground beef
1 large onion, chopped (1 cup)
1 15-ounce can Hunt's® Tomato Sauce
1 2¼-ounce can sliced pitted ripe olives, drained
1 1¼-ounce envelope taco seasoning mix
2 cups shredded cheddar cheese (8 ounces)
2 cups shredded lettuce
2 cups chopped tomatoes
1 8-ounce carton dairy sour cream

Prepare Cornmeal Pizza Dough. Grease two 11- to 13-inch pizza pans or large baking sheets. On lightly floured surface, roll each half of dough into circle 1 inch larger than pizza pan; transfer to pans. Build up edges slightly. Prick generously with fork. Do not let rise. Bake in 425° oven 10 to 12 minutes or until light brown. (If using refrigerated dough, press onto pans, then continue as above, *except* bake 8 to 10 minutes or until light brown.)

Meanwhile, in skillet cook beef and onion until meat is brown; drain. Stir in Hunt's Tomato Sauce, olives, and seasoning mix; heat through.

Spread beef mixture over hot crusts. Sprinkle with cheese. Bake 7 minutes or until cheese melts. Top with lettuce and tomatoes. Spoon on sour cream.

Cornmeal Pizza Dough: In bowl combine 1¼ cups all-purpose *flour*, 1 package active dry *yeast*, and ¼ teaspoon *salt*. Add 1 cup *warm water* (120° to 130°) and 2 tablespoons *Wesson® Oil*. Beat with electric mixer on low speed 30 seconds, scraping bowl constantly. Beat on high speed 3 minutes. Using spoon, stir in ¾ cup *yellow cornmeal* and as much of ¾ to 1¼ cups all-purpose *flour* as you can. Turn dough out onto lightly floured surface. Knead in enough remaining flour to make moderately stiff dough that is smooth and elastic (6 to 8 minutes total). Divide in half. Cover and let rest 10 minutes.

Nutrition facts per serving: 469 cal., 21 g pro., 44 g carbo., 25 g total fat (12 g sat. fat), 60 mg chol., 4 g dietary fiber, 1,107 mg sodium. Daily Value: 25% vit. A, 34% vit. C, 24% iron.

TIP-TOP TORTILLA ROLL-UPS

MAKES 6 SERVINGS
PREPARATION TIME: 10 MINUTES • COOKING TIME: 20 MINUTES

1 15-ounce can Hunt's® Ready Tomato Sauces Chunky Salsa	1 15-ounce can black beans or red kidney beans, rinsed and drained
1 14½-ounce can Hunt's® Choice-Cut™ Diced Tomatoes with Roasted Garlic	½ pound thinly sliced cooked beef, cut into strips
¾ cup quick-cooking brown rice	12 10-inch flour tortillas
½ cup water	Dairy sour cream or plain yogurt (optional)
½ teaspoon sugar	Sliced green onions (optional)
⅛ teaspoon pepper	

Reserve ½ *cup* Hunt's Ready Tomato Sauces Chunky Salsa. In skillet combine remaining salsa, *undrained* Hunt's Choice-Cut Diced Tomatoes with Roasted Garlic, *uncooked* rice, water, sugar, and pepper. Bring to boiling; reduce heat. Simmer, covered, 12 to 14 minutes or until rice is tender. Stir beans and beef into rice mixture. Simmer, uncovered, 5 minutes or until slightly thickened.

Meanwhile, wrap tortillas in foil. Heat in 350° oven 10 minutes.

Spoon rice mixture onto warm tortillas; roll up. Spoon reserved Hunt's Ready Tomato Sauces Chunky Salsa over tortillas. If desired, top with sour cream and green onions.

Nutrition facts per serving: 451 cal., 27 g pro., 68 g carbo., 9 g total fat (2 g sat. fat), 38 mg chol., 6 g dietary fiber, 1,263 mg sodium. Daily Value: 5% vit. A, 45% vit. C, 36% iron.

Fish Pancho Villa

Makes 4 Servings
Total Time: 20 Minutes

4 4-ounce fresh or frozen fish fillets,
½ inch thick
1 6-ounce can Hunt's® Tomato Paste
½ of a 1¼-ounce package taco
seasoning mix

1 tablespoon lime or lemon juice
2 cups quick-cooking rice
½ cup shredded Monterey Jack
cheese (2 ounces)

Thaw fish, if frozen. In skillet combine Hunt's Tomato Paste, seasoning mix, juice, and 2½ cups *water*. Bring to boiling. Add fish. Return to boiling; reduce heat. Simmer, covered, 4 to 6 minutes or until fish flakes easily with fork. Remove fish; keep warm. Bring tomato mixture to boiling. Add *uncooked* rice. Remove from heat. Cover; let stand 5 minutes. Fluff with fork. Serve fish over rice; sprinkle with cheese.

Nutrition facts per serving: 377 cal., 21 g pro., 50 g carbo., 7 g total fat (3 g sat. fat), 66 mg chol., 3 g dietary fiber, 730 mg sodium. Daily Value: 19% vit. A, 36% vit. C, 17% iron.

Mamma-Mia Minestrone Stew

Makes 5 Servings
Preparation Time: 10 Minutes • Cooking Time: 15 Minutes

1 large onion, chopped (1 cup)
1 teaspoon minced garlic (2 cloves)
1 tablespoon Wesson® Oil
3½ cups chicken broth
½ cup packaged dried corkscrew or
elbow macaroni
1 teaspoon dried Italian seasoning,
crushed

1 cup small broccoli flowerets
1 6-ounce can Hunt's® Tomato Paste
2 cups cubed cooked chicken
½ of a 15-ounce can (1 cup) red
kidney beans
Grated Parmesan cheese

Cook onion and garlic in hot Wesson Oil over medium heat 2 minutes. Carefully add broth, macaroni, and Italian seasoning. Bring to boiling; reduce heat. Simmer, covered, 7 minutes. Stir in broccoli and Hunt's Tomato Paste. Simmer, covered, 5 minutes or until pasta is tender. Add chicken and beans; heat through. Pass Parmesan cheese with stew.

Nutrition facts per serving: 254 cal., 19 g pro., 28 g carbo., 8 g total fat (2 g sat. fat), 20 mg chol., 5 g dietary fiber, 951 mg sodium. Daily Value: 17% vit. A, 63% vit. C, 22% iron.

BEST-YET OVEN BARBECUED CHICKEN

MAKES 4 TO 6 SERVINGS
PREPARATION TIME: 5 MINUTES • COOKING TIME: 55 MINUTES

1 **2½ to 3-pound broiler-fryer chicken, cut up**	1 **8-ounce can Hunt's® Tomato Sauce**
2 **tablespoons finely chopped onion**	2 **tablespoons cider vinegar or red wine vinegar**
2 **tablespoons Wesson® Oil**	1 **tablespoon brown sugar**
1 **16-ounce can whole cranberry sauce**	½ **to 1 teaspoon garlic salt**
	½ **teaspoon pepper**

In 3-quart rectangular baking dish arrange chicken. If desired, sprinkle chicken with salt and pepper. Bake in 425° oven 20 minutes. Reduce heat to 325° and bake 20 minutes more.

Meanwhile, in saucepan cook onion in hot Wesson Oil over medium heat 4 minutes or until tender. Stir in cranberry sauce, Hunt's Tomato Sauce, vinegar, brown sugar, garlic salt, and pepper. Bring to boiling; reduce heat. Simmer, uncovered, 10 minutes.

Remove chicken from oven; drain. Pour sauce mixture over chicken. Return to oven and bake 15 to 20 minutes more or until chicken is tender and no longer pink.

Nutrition facts per serving: 440 cal., 21 g pro., 51 g carbo., 17 g total fat (4 g sat. fat), 66 mg chol., 2 g dietary fiber, 706 mg sodium. Daily Value: 9% vit. A, 22% vit. C, 13% iron.

Tomato Paste Trick

Here's a slick way to quickly remove every rich, flavorful dab of Hunt's® Tomato Paste from the can. Using a can opener, open both ends of the can, then discard one end. Working over a bowl, use the other end to push against the paste to remove it easily and neatly from the can.

Just-Swell Stuffed Shells

Makes 8 Servings
Preparation Time: 30 Minutes • Cooking Time: 25 Minutes

16 packaged jumbo shell macaroni, cooked and drained
1 slightly beaten egg
2 cups shredded mozzarella cheese (8 ounces)
1 15-ounce container ricotta cheese

2 cups finely chopped cooked chicken, turkey, or ham
1 27½-ounce can Hunt's® Original Spaghetti Sauce Traditional
2 tablespoons grated Parmesan cheese

Invert cooked shells on paper towels; set aside. In bowl combine egg, mozzarella cheese, and ricotta cheese. Stir in chicken. Fill shells with cheese mixture.

Place shells in lightly greased 3-quart rectangular baking dish. Pour Hunt's Original Spaghetti Sauce Traditional over top. Sprinkle with Parmesan cheese. Bake, covered, in 425° oven 15 minutes. Uncover; bake 10 minutes more or until bubbly.

Nutrition facts per serving: 375 cal., 29 g pro., 28 g carbo., 17 g total fat (7 g sat. fat), 89 mg chol., 5 g dietary fiber, 1,043 mg sodium. Daily Value: 22% vit. A, 25% vit. C, 19% iron.

Side Dish Perfection—Anytime

When you keep several cans of Hunt's® Spaghetti Sauce on the cupboard shelf, it's easy to put together a top-notch side dish that complements broiled steaks, chops, burgers, poultry, or fish.

Simply warm the spaghetti sauce, spoon it over hot cooked spaghetti or other pasta, and sprinkle on some grated Parmesan cheese or shredded mozzarella cheese. For variety, use corkscrew macaroni or wagon-wheel pasta and stir cooked whole kernel corn or mixed vegetables into the sauce before you heat it.

A+ Turkey Lasagna

MAKES 8 SERVINGS
PREPARATION TIME: 25 MINUTES • COOKING TIME: 55 MINUTES

1 pound ground turkey sausage	2 cups Healthy Choice® Fat-Free Cottage Cheese, drained
1 27-ounce can Hunt's® Classic Italian Spaghetti Sauce with Tomato and Basil	½ cup grated Parmesan or Romano cheese
½ of a 6-ounce can (⅓ cup) Hunt's® Tomato Paste (see tip, below)	18 frozen lasagna strips
1 slightly beaten egg	3 cups shredded Healthy Choice® Mozzarella Cheese

In skillet cook sausage until brown; drain. Stir in Hunt's Classic Italian Spaghetti Sauce with Tomato and Basil and Hunt's Tomato Paste; heat through.

In bowl combine egg, Healthy Choice Cottage Cheese, and ¼ *cup* of the Parmesan cheese. In greased 3-quart rectangular baking dish arrange *one-third* of the frozen lasagna strips, trimming to fit. Spread *half* of the cottage cheese mixture over strips and top with *one-third* of the meat mixture. Sprinkle with *one-third* of the Healthy Choice Mozzarella Cheese. Repeat layers once.

Add remaining strips and meat mixture; sprinkle with remaining mozzarella cheese and Parmesan cheese. Bake, loosely covered, in 375° oven 45 minutes. Uncover; bake 10 to 15 minutes more or until hot. Let stand 10 minutes.

Nutrition facts per serving: 478 cal., 44 g pro., 47 g carbo., 10 g total fat (9 g sat. fat), 62 mg chol., 4 g dietary fiber, 1,567 mg sodium. Daily Value: 34% vit. A, 471% vit. C, 19% iron.

Freeze Extra Tomato Paste

If you have some Hunt's® Tomato Paste left over from a recipe, spoon 1-tablespoon mounds into freezer bags and freeze. Then you'll have small portions ready to use the next time a recipe calls for a tablespoon or two of paste. Or, boost the flavor of soup or sauce by stirring in a portion.

Cornmeal-Topped Turkey Pie

Makes 6 Servings
Preparation Time: 25 Minutes • Cooking Time: 25 Minutes

1¼ cups cold water	1 medium green sweet pepper, chopped (¾ cup)
½ cup yellow cornmeal	1 15-ounce can Hunt's® Ready Tomato Sauces Chunky Chili
1 tablespoon margarine or butter	
¼ teaspoon salt	½ cup Hunt's® Tomato Juice
⅛ teaspoon black pepper	1 tablespoon yellow cornmeal
1 pound ground raw turkey or lean ground beef	½ cup shredded Healthy Choice® Cheddar Cheese (2 ounces)

In saucepan combine cold water, ½ cup cornmeal, margarine, salt, and black pepper. Bring just to boiling; reduce heat. Cook, uncovered, over low heat 5 minutes, stirring often. (Mixture will be thick.) Remove from heat. Set aside.

Meanwhile, in skillet cook turkey and sweet pepper until meat is brown; drain. Stir in Hunt's Ready Tomato Sauces Chunky Chili, Hunt's Tomato Juice, and 1 tablespoon cornmeal; bring to boiling.

Spoon hot turkey mixture into 2-quart rectangular baking dish. Spoon cornmeal mixture into 6 mounds on top.

Bake, uncovered, in 375° oven 25 minutes or until bubbly. Immediately sprinkle with Healthy Choice Cheddar Cheese. Let stand 2 to 3 minutes or until cheese melts.

Nutrition facts per serving: 203 cal., 15 g pro., 18 g carbo., 8 g total fat (2 g sat. fat), 17 mg chol., 2 g dietary fiber, 652 mg sodium. Daily Value: 21% vit. A, 25% vit. C, 12% iron.

COWBOY EGGS AND MUFFINS

MAKES 4 SERVINGS
TOTAL TIME: 15 MINUTES

1 15-ounce can Hunt's® Ready Tomato Sauces Chunky Tomato	½ cup chopped green or red sweet pepper
4 eggs	1 cup chopped cooked chicken
¼ cup milk	4 English muffins, split and toasted
⅛ teaspoon salt	Cheddar cheese triangles (optional)
⅛ teaspoon black pepper	
2 tablespoons margarine or butter	

In saucepan heat Hunt's Ready Tomato Sauces Chunky Tomato to boiling, stirring occasionally. Cover; keep warm.

Meanwhile, in bowl beat together eggs, milk, salt, and black pepper; set aside. In skillet melt margarine over medium heat; add sweet pepper and cook until tender. Stir in chicken; pour egg mixture over top. Cook and stir until eggs are cooked throughout but still glossy and moist. Remove from heat. Spoon over muffins; top with warm tomato sauce, and, if desired, cheese triangles.

Nutrition facts per serving: 369 cal., 23 g pro., 34 g carbo., 15 g total fat (4 g sat. fat), 248 mg chol., 2 g dietary fiber, 1,187 mg sodium. Daily Value: 29% vit. A, 41% vit. C, 18% iron.

Cooked Chicken Options

Leftover roasted or broiled chicken works well in the recipe above. If you don't have leftover chicken, you can buy frozen cooked chicken or quickly poach a chicken breast.

To poach the chicken, place it in a skillet with 1 cup water. Bring to boiling; reduce heat. Simmer, covered, 12 to 14 minutes or until tender and no longer pink. Drain and chop. Six ounces of skinless, boneless chicken yields about 1 cup chopped cooked chicken.

INTERNATIONAL FAVORITES

Sample the recipes in this section and everyone will be drawn to the aromas of international cooking coming from your kitchen. Whether you're in the mood for something from south of the border or from sunny Italy, these specialties will satisfy your craving. Best of all, Hunt's® Ready Tomato Sauces add simmered-to-perfection flavor to every dish.

Beef and Broccoli Stir-Fry
(see recipe, page 44)

BEEF AND BROCCOLI STIR-FRY

MAKES 4 SERVINGS
TOTAL TIME: 35 MINUTES

1   15-ounce can Hunt's® Ready
    Tomato Sauces Chunky Special
2   tablespoons La Choy® Soy Sauce
1   tablespoon cornstarch
¼   to ½ teaspoon ground ginger
3   tablespoons Wesson® Oil
1½ cups broccoli flowerets or red
    and/or green sweet pepper
    strips*
1   cup sliced fresh mushrooms

6   green onions, cut into ¾-inch
    pieces
½   teaspoon minced garlic (1 clove)
1   pound beef top round steak, cut
    into thin, bite-size strips
    (see tip, page 48)
    Crushed red pepper (optional)
2   cups hot cooked rice
    Toasted pine nuts (optional)

In bowl combine Hunt's Ready Tomato Sauces Chunky Special, La Choy Soy Sauce, cornstarch, and ginger; set aside.

In skillet heat *1 tablespoon* Wesson Oil over medium-high heat. Add broccoli or sweet pepper, mushrooms, green onions, and garlic. Stir-fry 2 to 3 minutes or until vegetables are crisp-tender. Remove with slotted spoon.

Add remaining oil to skillet. Stir-fry meat, *half* at a time, 2 to 3 minutes or until desired doneness. Return all meat to skillet; push to sides of pan. Stir tomato sauce mixture and add to skillet. Cook and stir until thickened and bubbly. Return cooked vegetables to skillet. Cook and stir 2 minutes more. If desired, season to taste with crushed red pepper. Serve over rice. If desired, sprinkle with pine nuts.

*Note: If desired, substitute one 10-ounce package frozen chopped green sweet peppers, thawed, for fresh pepper strips. Instead of cooking frozen peppers with mushrooms, add them when returning cooked vegetables to skillet.

Nutrition facts per serving: 459 cal., 34 g pro., 43 g carbo., 18 g total fat (3 g sat. fat), 72 mg chol., 4 g dietary fiber, 1,047 mg sodium. Daily Value: 31% vit. A, 99% vit. C, 30% iron.

SUPER CHUNKY PASTA SAUCE

MAKES 4 TO 6 SERVINGS
PREPARATION TIME: 20 MINUTES • COOKING TIME: 17 MINUTES

1   pound ground beef
1½ cups sliced fresh mushrooms
1   large green sweet pepper,
    chopped (1 cup)
1   medium onion, chopped (½ cup)
1   15-ounce can Hunt's® Ready
    Tomato Sauces Chunky Garlic
    and Herb
1   14½-ounce can Hunt's® Choice-
    Cut™ Diced Tomatoes

½   of a 6-ounce can (⅓ cup) Hunt's®
    Tomato Paste (see tip, page 38)
2   tablespoons snipped fresh parsley
½   pound packaged dried mostaccioli
    or fettuccine, cooked and
    drained
2   tablespoons freshly grated
    Parmesan cheese

In skillet cook ground beef, mushrooms, sweet pepper, and onion until meat is brown; drain. Stir in Hunt's Ready Tomato Sauces Chunky Garlic and Herb, *undrained* Hunt's Choice-Cut Diced Tomatoes, and Hunt's Tomato Paste.

Bring to boiling; reduce heat. Simmer, uncovered, 12 to 15 minutes or until desired consistency, stirring occasionally. Stir in parsley. Serve over mostaccioli. Sprinkle with Parmesan cheese.

Note: Pictured on the cover.

Nutrition facts per serving: 564 cal., 33 g pro., 68 g carbo., 18 g total fat (7 g sat. fat), 72 mg chol., 4 g dietary fiber, 964 mg sodium. Daily Value: 20% vit. A, 117% vit. C, 43% iron.

Timesaving Tomatoes

Save time with Hunt's® Choice-Cut™ Diced Tomatoes. Anytime a recipe lists cut-up whole tomatoes as one of the ingredients, you can substitute diced tomatoes. They're an easy way to add rich tomato flavor to all types of dishes. Choose from the three delicious types—Original, with Italian Style Herbs, and with Roasted Garlic.

PORK PAPRIKASH

MAKES 4 SERVINGS
PREPARATION TIME: 20 MINUTES • COOKING TIME: 45 MINUTES

1 pound lean boneless pork, cut into ¾-inch pieces	1 large green sweet pepper, cut into 1-inch squares
1 tablespoon **Wesson®** Oil	1 cup frozen small whole onions
½ cup water	1 4½-ounce jar whole mushrooms, drained
2 teaspoons paprika	
1 teaspoon instant beef bouillon granules	1 8-ounce carton dairy sour cream
	1 tablespoon all-purpose flour
1 15-ounce can **Hunt's®** Ready Tomato Sauces Original Italian	2 cups hot cooked noodles or spaetzle

In 12-inch skillet cook pork, *half* at a time, in hot Wesson Oil over medium-high heat until brown; drain. Return all of the pork to skillet. Add water, paprika, and bouillon granules. Bring to boiling; reduce heat. Simmer, covered, 20 minutes.

Stir in Hunt's Ready Tomato Sauces Original Italian, sweet pepper, onions, and mushrooms. Return to boiling; reduce heat. Simmer, covered, 15 minutes more or until meat and vegetables are tender. Combine sour cream and flour; add to skillet. Cook and stir until thickened and bubbly. Cook and stir 1 minute more. Serve over noodles.

Nutrition facts per serving: 476 cal., 26 g pro., 39 g carbo., 25 g total fat (11 g sat. fat), 103 mg chol., 5 g dietary fiber, 642 mg sodium. Daily Value: 37% vit. A, 45% vit. C, 24% iron.

Add Zip to Sauces and Soups

Hunt's® Ready Tomato Sauces are ideal ways to add ethnic flavor to just about any soup, stew, or spaghetti sauce. For Italian-seasoned dishes, use Hunt's Ready Tomato Sauces Chunky or Original Italian. For Mexican flair, try Hunt's Ready Tomato Sauces Chunky Chili or Chunky Salsa. For Mediterranean panache, use Hunt's Ready Tomato Sauces Chunky Garlic and Herb.

PORK AND ZUCCHINI PARMIGIANA

MAKES 6 SERVINGS
PREPARATION TIME: 25 MINUTES • COOKING TIME: 10 MINUTES

¾   pound lean boneless pork or lamb, partially frozen
1   tablespoon Wesson® Oil
1   small onion, chopped (⅓ cup)
1   15-ounce can Hunt's® Ready Tomato Sauces Chunky Garlic and Herb

¼   cup Hunt's® Tomato Paste (see tip, page 38)
3   cups zucchini sliced ¼ inch thick
1½   cups shredded mozzarella cheese (6 ounces)
½   cup grated Parmesan or Romano cheese

Thinly slice meat across grain into bite-size strips. In skillet heat Wesson Oil over medium-high heat. Add pork and onion. Stir-fry 3 to 4 minutes or until pork is no longer pink. Stir in Hunt's Ready Tomato Sauces Chunky Garlic and Herb and Hunt's Tomato Paste. Bring to boiling.

Meanwhile, in steamer basket steam zucchini over simmering water 5 minutes. In lightly greased 2-quart rectangular baking dish arrange *half* of the zucchini; spoon *half* of the pork mixture over. Sprinkle with *half* of the mozzarella cheese and *half* of the Parmesan cheese. Repeat layers. Bake, covered, in 425° oven 10 to 12 minutes or until heated through.

Nutrition facts per serving: 256 cal., 20 g pro., 14 g carbo., 13 g total fat (6 g sat. fat), 48 mg chol., 2 g dietary fiber, 552 mg sodium. Daily Value: 13% vit. A, 38% vit. C, 11% iron.

Slicing It Thin

Slicing meat into thin strips for quick cooking in stir-fries or other recipes, such as the one above, is much easier if the meat is partially frozen until it's firm. Place the meat in the freezer about 30 minutes while you prepare the other ingredients, and then slice it. If you want extremely thin slices, freeze the meat 45 to 60 minutes before slicing.

ITALIAN SAUSAGE-STUFFED EGGPLANT

MAKES 4 SERVINGS
PREPARATION TIME: 30 MINUTES • COOKING TIME: 50 MINUTES

2 small eggplants (about ¾ pound each)
¾ pound bulk mild Italian sausage
1 medium onion, chopped (½ cup)
1 small green sweet pepper, chopped (½ cup)
½ teaspoon minced garlic (1 clove)
1 8-ounce can Hunt's® Tomato Sauce

¼ cup fine dry seasoned bread crumbs
3 tablespoons grated Parmesan cheese
¼ teaspoon black pepper
1 cup shredded mozzarella cheese (4 ounces)

Cut each eggplant in half lengthwise. Scoop out and reserve pulp, leaving ¼-inch-thick shells. Place shells in 3-quart rectangular baking dish. Finely chop pulp; set aside.

In skillet cook sausage, onion, sweet pepper, and garlic until meat is brown; drain. Stir in reserved eggplant pulp, Hunt's Tomato Sauce, bread crumbs, Parmesan cheese, and black pepper. Divide among shells.

Bake, covered, in 350° oven 45 minutes or until eggplant is tender. Sprinkle with mozzarella cheese. Bake, uncovered, 5 minutes more or until cheese melts.

Nutrition facts per serving: 390 cal., 25 g pro., 23 g carbo., 23 g total fat (9 g sat. fat), 68 mg chol., 6 g dietary fiber, 1,337 mg sodium. Daily Value: 13% vit. A, 36% vit. C, 15% iron.

Watching Your Salt

Are you concerned about the amount of sodium in the dishes you serve your family? If you are, take advantage of Hunt's® No-Salt-Added products. For delicious lower-sodium dishes, use the no-salt-added versions of whole tomatoes, tomato sauce, tomato paste, stewed tomatoes, and tomato juice in place of the regular products called for in your recipes. Then, if you like, increase the other seasonings slightly.

LINGUINE WITH RED CLAM SAUCE

MAKES 4 SERVINGS
PREPARATION TIME: 15 MINUTES • COOKING TIME: 5 MINUTES

2 6½-ounce cans chopped clams	1 tablespoon snipped fresh parsley
1 medium onion, chopped (½ cup)	½ teaspoon dried thyme, crushed
2½ teaspoons minced garlic (5 cloves)	⅛ teaspoon pepper
1 tablespoon Wesson® Oil	8 ounces packaged dried linguine,
1 15-ounce can Hunt's® Ready	cooked and drained
Tomato Sauces Original Italian	¼ cup grated Parmesan cheese

Drain clams, reserving ¼ *cup* liquid. In skillet cook clams, onion, and garlic in hot Wesson Oil until onion is tender.

Stir in reserved clam liquid, Hunt's Ready Tomato Sauces Original Italian, parsley, thyme, and pepper. If desired, season to taste with salt. Heat through. Spoon over linguine. Sprinkle with Parmesan cheese.

Nutrition facts per serving: 395 cal., 22 g pro., 60 g carbo., 8 g total fat (2 g sat. fat), 29 mg chol., 3 g dietary fiber, 615 mg sodium. Daily Value: 25% vit. A, 35% vit. C, 104% iron.

Spur-of-the-Moment Meal

Keep the Hunt's® Ready Tomato Sauces Original Italian, canned clams, and dried linguine used in this flavorful recipe on hand for any time you need a quick dinner. The clam sauce is easy to make in only 20 minutes. Round out the meal with a vegetable, tossed salad, and sliced French bread or crunchy bread sticks.

SOUTH-OF-FRANCE SOLE

MAKES 4 SERVINGS
PREPARATION TIME: 25 MINUTES • COOKING TIME: 30 MINUTES

1 pound fresh or frozen sole fillets, ¼ to ½ inch thick	¼ cup snipped fresh parsley
1 medium onion, chopped (½ cup)	¼ cup dry white wine or chicken broth
1 stalk celery, sliced (½ cup)	2 teaspoons lemon juice
1 teaspoon minced garlic (2 cloves)	½ teaspoon sugar
2 tablespoons Wesson® Oil	½ teaspoon salt
1 15-ounce can Hunt's® Tomato Sauce	½ teaspoon dried Italian seasoning, crushed
1 4½-ounce jar sliced mushrooms, drained	⅛ teaspoon pepper
	Hot cooked rice (optional)

Thaw fish, if frozen. In skillet cook onion, celery, and garlic in hot Wesson Oil over medium heat until vegetables are tender. Stir in Hunt's Tomato Sauce, mushrooms, parsley, wine, lemon juice, sugar, salt, Italian seasoning, and pepper.

Bring to boiling; reduce heat. Simmer, covered, 20 minutes, stirring occasionally. Add fish; spoon tomato mixture over top. Cook, covered, 5 to 7 minutes more or until fish flakes easily with fork. If desired, serve over rice.

Nutrition facts per serving: 218 cal., 21 g pro., 12 g carbo., 8 g total fat (1 g sat. fat), 53 mg chol., 3 g dietary fiber, 1,158 mg sodium. Daily Value: 13% vit. A, 41% vit. C, 14% iron.

Fish Finesse

Judging when fish is done sometimes can be tricky. For best results, cook the fish until it is opaque. Then test it for doneness by inserting the tines of a fork into the fish and twisting gently. The fish should just begin to flake easily. Any juices should be milky white. If the fish is translucent and the juices still are clear, cook a few minutes longer.

CHICKEN WITH POLENTA

MAKES 6 SERVINGS
PREPARATION TIME: 15 MINUTES • COOKING TIME: 1 HOUR 35 MINUTES

1 3- to 3½-pound broiler-fryer chicken	¼ teaspoon salt
1 tablespoon **Wesson®** Oil	Polenta (see recipe below)
½ teaspoon minced garlic (1 clove)	1 tablespoon grated Parmesan or Romano cheese
½ teaspoon dried basil, crushed	1 15-ounce can **Hunt's®** Ready Tomato Sauces Chunky Italian
½ teaspoon dried oregano, crushed	

Skewer neck skin of chicken to back; tie legs to tail. Twist wings under back. Place chicken on rack in roasting pan. Brush with Wesson Oil. Spread garlic over chicken, then rub with basil, oregano, and salt. Roast, uncovered, in 375° oven 1¼ to 1½ hours or until chicken is no longer pink and meat thermometer inserted in center of inside thigh muscle registers 180° to 185°. Baste occasionally with pan juices.

Meanwhile, prepare Polenta. Remove chicken from oven; cover and keep warm. Bake Polenta in 375° oven 20 minutes or until heated through; sprinkle Parmesan cheese over top. In saucepan bring Hunt's Ready Tomato Sauces Chunky Italian to boiling; reduce heat. Simmer, uncovered, 5 minutes. Serve with chicken and Polenta.

Polenta: In saucepan bring 2¾ cups *chicken broth* to boiling. In bowl combine 1 cup *cornmeal*, 1 cup *cold water*, and dash *salt*. Slowly add to boiling broth, stirring constantly. Cook and stir until mixture returns to boiling; reduce heat. Cook, uncovered, over low heat 10 to 15 minutes or until very thick, stirring occasionally. Pour into 9-inch pie plate. Cover and refrigerate 30 minutes or until firm.

Nutrition facts per serving: 376 cal., 30 g pro., 24 g carbo., 17 g total fat (4 g sat. fat), 80 mg chol., 3 g dietary fiber, 891 mg sodium. Daily Value: 10% vit. A, 2% vit. C, 18% iron.

BASQUE-STYLE CHICKEN

MAKES 4 SERVINGS
PREPARATION TIME: 30 MINUTES • COOKING TIME: 35 MINUTES

4 large chicken breast halves or drumstick-thigh pieces (about 2 pounds total)	½ cup dry white wine or chicken broth
2 tablespoons **Wesson® Oil**	¼ teaspoon salt
2 cups fresh mushrooms, halved	¼ teaspoon black pepper
2 medium sweet peppers (red, green, or yellow), cut into strips	¼ cup cold water
I medium onion, sliced	**2** tablespoons cornstarch
I 14½-ounce can **Hunt's® Choice-Cut™ Diced Tomatoes with Italian Style Herbs**	**I** cup loose-pack frozen peas
	2 cups hot cooked rice

Skin chicken. In 12-inch skillet cook chicken in hot Wesson Oil over medium heat 10 minutes or until light brown, turning to brown evenly. Remove chicken. Add mushrooms, sweet peppers, and onion to skillet. Cook and stir 3 minutes.

Stir in *undrained* Hunt's Choice-Cut Diced Tomatoes with Italian Style Herbs, wine, salt, and black pepper. Bring to boiling; reduce heat. Return chicken to skillet; if desired, sprinkle with additional salt and black pepper. Simmer, covered, 25 to 30 minutes or until chicken is tender and no longer pink. Transfer chicken to platter. Cover; keep warm.

Skim any fat from vegetable mixture. Combine water and cornstarch; stir into vegetable mixture. Stir in peas. Cook and stir until thickened and bubbly. Cook and stir 2 minutes more. Spoon over chicken and rice.

Nutrition facts per serving: 461 cal., 33 g pro., 42 g carbo., 16 g total fat (3 g sat. fat), 90 mg chol., 3 g dietary fiber, 787 mg sodium. Daily Value: 38% vit. A, 139% vit. C, 26% iron.

EASY CHICKEN CASSOULET

MAKES 6 SERVINGS
PREPARATION TIME: 25 MINUTES • COOKING TIME: 40 MINUTES

½ pound bulk pork sausage
1 medium onion, chopped (½ cup)
2 pounds meaty chicken pieces
   (breasts, thighs, and drumsticks)
1 15-ounce can Hunt's® Ready
   Tomato Sauces Chunky Garlic
   and Herb

1 10-ounce package frozen lima
   beans
1 cup fresh or frozen cut green
   beans
1 bay leaf
½ teaspoon salt
¼ teaspoon pepper

In 12-inch skillet cook sausage and onion until meat is brown; drain, reserving 2 tablespoons drippings in skillet. Set sausage mixture aside. If desired, skin chicken. Cook chicken in reserved drippings 10 minutes or until light brown, turning to brown evenly; drain.

Return sausage mixture to skillet. Stir in Hunt's Ready Tomato Sauces Chunky Garlic and Herb, lima beans, green beans, bay leaf, salt, and pepper. Bring to boiling; reduce heat. Simmer, covered, 35 minutes or until chicken is tender and no longer pink. Discard bay leaf.

Nutrition facts per serving: 419 cal., 36 g pro., 35 g carbo., 15 g total fat (4 g sat. fat), 84 mg chol., 5 g dietary fiber, 687 mg sodium. Daily Value: 6% vit. A, 31% vit. C, 33% iron.

Poultry Pointers

When handling chicken or other poultry, food experts have a few safety pointers:

- Refrigerate raw chicken promptly. Don't leave it at room temperature for any length of time.

- Before cooking chicken, rinse it under cold running water and pat dry with paper towels.

- After handling raw chicken, be sure to wash your hands before touching other foods. Also wash countertops, cutting boards, plates, and any utensils you've used.

- Don't leave cooked chicken at room temperature for more than 2 hours. Cover and refrigerate it promptly.

MOZZARELLA-TOPPED TURKEY AND EGGPLANT

MAKES 4 SERVINGS
TOTAL TIME: 30 MINUTES

1 small eggplant, cut into 1-inch cubes (about 4 cups)	4 turkey breast tenderloin steaks or medium skinless, boneless chicken breast halves (about 1 pound total)
1 14½-ounce can vegetable or chicken broth	
⅔ cup packaged dried orzo (rosamarina)	1 tablespoon Wesson® Oil
¼ teaspoon pepper	½ cup shredded Healthy Choice® Mozzarella Cheese (2 ounces)
1 15-ounce can Hunt's® Ready Tomato Sauces Chunky Italian	

In saucepan combine eggplant, broth, orzo, and pepper. Bring to boiling; reduce heat. Simmer, covered, 12 to 15 minutes or until orzo is tender. Stir in Hunt's Ready Tomato Sauces Chunky Italian. Cook, covered, 5 minutes more.

Meanwhile, in skillet cook turkey in hot Wesson Oil over medium-high heat 10 to 12 minutes or until turkey is tender and no longer pink, turning once.

Serve turkey on orzo mixture. Top with Healthy Choice Mozzarella Cheese.

Nutrition facts per serving: 346 cal., 32 g pro., 37 g carbo., 9 g total fat (1 g sat. fat), 52 mg chol., 4 g dietary fiber, 1,071 mg sodium. Daily Value: 16% vit. A, 5% vit. C, 20% iron.

UNFORGETTABLE VEGETABLE-STUFFED MANICOTTI

MAKES 5 SERVINGS
PREPARATION TIME: 40 MINUTES • COOKING TIME: 30 MINUTES

10 packaged dried manicotti shells, cooked and drained	1 cup finely chopped fresh mushrooms
2 15-ounce cans Hunt's® Ready Tomato Sauces Original Italian	1 cup finely chopped fresh broccoli
1 slightly beaten egg	1 cup shredded mozzarella cheese (4 ounces)
1 15-ounce carton ricotta cheese	1 medium carrot, shredded (½ cup)
	¼ cup grated Parmesan cheese

Rinse cooked manicotti with cold water; drain again.

Meanwhile, for sauce, in saucepan bring Hunt's Ready Tomato Sauces Original Italian to boiling; reduce heat. Simmer, uncovered, 10 minutes, stirring occasionally. Remove from heat; set aside.

For filling, in bowl combine egg, ricotta cheese, mushrooms, broccoli, mozzarella cheese, carrot, and Parmesan cheese. Using small spoon, fill *each* manicotti with a generous ¼ *cup* filling.

Spread sauce in 3-quart rectangular baking dish. Place manicotti on top of sauce. Bake, covered, in 350° oven 30 to 35 minutes or until bubbly.

Nutrition facts per serving: 441 cal., 28 g pro., 49 g carbo., 16 g total fat (9 g sat. fat), 90 mg chol., 6 g dietary fiber, 1,028 mg sodium. Daily Value: 83% vit. A, 57% vit. C, 26% iron.

Spicy Tex-Mex Drumettes

MAKES 10 APPETIZER SERVINGS
PREPARATION TIME: 20 MINUTES • MARINATING TIME: 2 HOURS
COOKING TIME: 40 MINUTES

- 1 16-ounce package chicken drumettes (about 20 pieces) or 10 chicken wings
- 1 8-ounce can Hunt's® Tomato Sauce
- 2 to 4 tablespoons bottled hot pepper sauce

- 2 tablespoons Wesson® Oil
- 1 tablespoon lime juice
- 1 tablespoon La Choy® Soy Sauce
- 1 teaspoon garlic powder
- ½ teaspoon ground cumin

Place drumettes in plastic bag set in deep bowl. (Or, if using wings, cut off and discard tips. Cut wings at joints to form 20 pieces. Place in bag set in bowl.)

For marinade, in bowl combine Hunt's Tomato Sauce, pepper sauce, Wesson Oil, lime juice, La Choy Soy Sauce, garlic powder, and cumin. Pour over chicken. Seal bag. Refrigerate 2 to 4 hours, turning bag occasionally.

Drain chicken, reserving marinade. Place chicken in greased, foil-lined 15x10x1-inch baking pan. Bake in 375° oven 30 minutes. Turn chicken over; pour marinade over top. Bake 10 to 15 minutes more or until tender and no longer pink.

Nutrition facts per serving: 133 cal., 10 g pro., 2 g carbo., 9 g total fat (2 g sat. fat), 29 mg chol., 0 g dietary fiber, 286 mg sodium. Daily Value: 4% vit. A, 9% vit. C, 5% iron.

Sensational Mango Salsa,
Spicy Tex-Mex Drumettes

Sensational Mango Salsa

Makes 16 Appetizer Servings
Preparation Time: 25 Minutes • Chilling Time: 1 Hour

1 14½-ounce can Hunt's® Choice-Cut™ Diced Tomatoes
2 ripe medium mangos, peeled and finely chopped
½ cup finely snipped fresh cilantro
2 tablespoons finely chopped onion

2 tablespoons lime juice
2 tablespoons tequila
2 teaspoons minced garlic (4 cloves)
½ teaspoon salt
½ teaspoon ground cumin
½ teaspoon pepper

In bowl combine *undrained* Hunt's Choice-Cut Diced Tomatoes and remaining ingredients. Cover and refrigerate at least 1 hour. Serve with tortilla chips.

Nutrition facts per serving: 28 cal., 0 g pro., 6 g carbo., 0 g total fat (0 g sat. fat), 0 mg chol., 1 g dietary fiber, 181 mg sodium. Daily Value: 12% vit. A, 19% vit. C, 1% iron.

Snappy Salsa Dip

Makes 16 Appetizer Servings
Preparation Time: 10 Minutes • Cooking Time: 5 Minutes

1 pound ground beef
3 cups shredded cheddar cheese (12 ounces) or 1½ cups shredded cheddar cheese (6 ounces) plus 1½ cups shredded Monterey Jack cheese with jalapeño peppers (6 ounces)

1 15-ounce can Hunt's® Ready Tomato Sauces Chunky Salsa
Dash bottled hot pepper sauce (optional)

In skillet cook beef until brown; drain. Stir in cheese, Hunt's Ready Tomato Sauces Chunky Salsa, and, if desired, pepper sauce. Cook and stir over low heat until warm. Serve warm with tortilla chips.

Nutrition facts per serving: 150 cal., 12 g pro., 2 g carbo., 11 g total fat (6 g sat. fat), 40 mg chol., 0 g dietary fiber, 285 mg sodium. Daily Value: 6% vit. A, 10% vit. C, 5% iron.

READY, SET, SERVE

Even when you have a busy week ahead, you can bring 'em home for dinner every night with these make-ahead dishes. They're the perfect answer when cooking is out of the question. With a little advance preparation and Hunt's® flavor-packed tomato products, you'll be ready for any occasion. Make this a routine and dinnertime will become a time to relax and enjoy great food with your family.

Ham-Stuffed Chicken Rolls
(see recipe, page 64)

HAM-STUFFED CHICKEN ROLLS

MAKES 4 SERVINGS
PREPARATION TIME: 35 MINUTES • CHILLING TIME: 8 HOURS
COOKING TIME: 30 MINUTES

½ cup diced fully cooked ham
½ cup shredded mozzarella cheese (2 ounces)
2 tablespoons snipped fresh parsley
¼ teaspoon dried marjoram or thyme, crushed

4 medium skinless, boneless chicken breast halves
1 tablespoon **Wesson®** Oil
1 15-ounce can Hunt's® Ready Tomato Sauces Chunky Special
2 cups hot cooked orzo (rosamarina) or rice

For filling, in bowl combine ham, mozzarella cheese, parsley, and marjoram. Set aside.

Place each chicken half between 2 pieces of plastic wrap. Pound each lightly with flat side of meat mallet to form ⅛-inch-thick rectangle. Remove plastic wrap. Place about ¼ cup filling on each rectangle. Roll up jelly-roll style, folding in sides as you roll. Secure with wooden toothpicks.* Cover and refrigerate 8 to 24 hours.

To serve, in skillet cook chicken rolls on all sides in hot Wesson Oil until brown; drain. Add Hunt's Ready Tomato Sauces Chunky Special. Bring to boiling; reduce heat. Simmer, covered, 20 to 25 minutes or until chicken is tender and no longer pink. Remove toothpicks. Serve over orzo.

*__Note: To serve immediately,__ at this point, omit chilling chicken rolls. Continue cooking as directed.

Nutrition facts per serving: 353 cal., 33 g pro., 29 g carbo., 12 g total fat (3 g sat. fat), 77 mg chol., 3 g dietary fiber, 797 mg sodium. Daily Value: 24% vit. A, 36% vit. C, 12% iron.

Easy Meals on Call

Make-ahead cooking is today's solution for busy families who want to enjoy home-cooked, heartwarming meals together. Use any of the recipes in this chapter to ease your before-dinner time-crunch by preparing them ahead as directed. When mealtime rolls around, you can have a delicious main dish ready with next to no effort. These recipes make on-call meals easy, and Hunt's® products make them taste terrific.

TOMATO-SAUCED TURKEY

MAKES 4 SERVINGS
PREPARATION TIME: 20 MINUTES • FREEZING TIME: UP TO 3 MONTHS
COOKING TIME: 70 MINUTES

3½ ounces packaged dried fine
     noodles (2 cups), cooked and
     drained
¾   pound turkey breast tenderloin
     steaks or skinless, boneless
     chicken breast halves
1   tablespoon Wesson® Oil

1   15-ounce can Hunt's® Ready
     Tomato Sauces Chunky Special
1   8-ounce can Hunt's® Tomato
     Sauce
1   4½-ounce jar sliced mushrooms,
     drained
⅛   teaspoon pepper
¾   cup frozen small whole onions

Rinse cooked noodles with cold water.* Drain; set aside.

Meanwhile, thinly slice turkey into bite-size strips. In skillet cook and stir turkey in hot Wesson Oil over medium heat 3 to 4 minutes or until no longer pink. Remove from skillet.

Add Hunt's Ready Tomato Sauces Chunky Special, Hunt's Tomato Sauce, mushrooms, and pepper to skillet. Cook and stir over medium heat until heated through. Remove from heat; stir in onions and turkey.

Spoon noodles into 4 individual shallow baking dishes. Spoon turkey mixture over. Cover with plastic wrap, then foil. Label and freeze up to 3 months.

To serve, remove plastic wrap. Cover loosely with foil. Bake in 375° oven 70 minutes or until heated through.

*Note: To serve immediately, do not rinse cooked noodles with cold water. Then, add onions to skillet with mushrooms. Bring to boiling, reduce heat, and simmer, covered, 5 minutes or until onions are tender. Add turkey and heat through.

Nutrition facts per serving: 292 cal., 22 g pro., 35 g carbo., 8 g total fat (1 g sat. fat), 55 mg chol., 4 g dietary fiber, 979 mg sodium. Daily Value: 26% vit. A, 44% vit. C, 16% iron.

FISH WITH GAZPACHO SAUCE

MAKES 6 SERVINGS
PREPARATION TIME: 20 MINUTES • CHILLING TIME: 2 HOURS
COOKING TIME: 4 MINUTES

1 **14½-ounce can Hunt's® Choice-** **Cut™ Diced Tomatoes**	½ **teaspoon sugar**
½ **cup chopped seeded cucumber**	⅛ **teaspoon garlic powder**
¼ **cup chopped green sweet pepper**	**Dash black pepper**
2 **green onions, thinly sliced**	1½ **pounds fresh or frozen cod,**
2 **tablespoons cider vinegar or red**	**haddock, or orange roughy**
wine vinegar	**fillets, ½ inch thick**
1 **tablespoon Wesson® Oil**	½ **teaspoon lemon-pepper seasoning**
	Snipped fresh cilantro

For sauce, in bowl combine *undrained* Hunt's Choice-Cut Diced Tomatoes, cucumber, sweet pepper, green onions, vinegar, Wesson Oil, sugar, garlic powder, and black pepper. Cover and refrigerate 2 to 24 hours.

To serve, thaw fish, if frozen. Cut fish into 6 serving-size portions. Sprinkle with lemon-pepper seasoning. Place on unheated rack of broiler pan; tuck under any thin portions. Broil 3 to 4 inches from heat 4 to 6 minutes or until fish flakes easily with fork. Transfer fish to platter. Sprinkle with cilantro. Serve sauce with fish.

Note: If desired, stir additional cilantro into any remaining sauce, then cover and refrigerate for up to 3 days. Serve with tortilla chips.

Nutrition facts per serving: 119 cal., 19 g pro., 4 g carbo., 3 g total fat (0 g sat. fat), 43 mg chol., 1 g dietary fiber, 455 mg sodium. Daily Value: 7% vit. A, 33% vit. C, 3% iron.

WHITE BEAN AND SAUSAGE RIGATONI

MAKES 4 SERVINGS
PREPARATION TIME: 25 MINUTES • CHILLING TIME: 8 HOURS
COOKING TIME: 45 MINUTES

½ **pound packaged dried rigatoni (5 cups)**

2 **14½-ounce cans Hunt's® Choice-Cut™ Diced Tomatoes with Italian Style Herbs**

1 **15-ounce can great northern beans, drained**

½ **pound fully cooked turkey kielbasa, bias sliced**

½ **of a 10-ounce package frozen chopped spinach, thawed and well drained**

½ **of a 6-ounce can (⅓ cup) Hunt's® Tomato Paste (see tip, page 38)**

¼ **cup dry red wine or reduced-sodium chicken broth**

¼ **cup finely shredded or grated Parmesan cheese**

Cook and drain rigatoni. In large bowl combine cooked rigatoni, *undrained* Hunt's Choice-Cut Diced Tomatoes with Italian Style Herbs, beans, kielbasa, spinach, Hunt's Tomato Paste, and wine. Spoon into 2-quart round casserole.* Cover with plastic wrap, then foil. Refrigerate 8 to 24 hours.

To serve, remove plastic wrap. Stir once. Cover loosely with foil. Bake in 375° oven 55 to 65 minutes or until heated through. Sprinkle with Parmesan cheese.

***Note: To serve immediately,** at this point, sprinkle with Parmesan cheese. Bake, uncovered, in 375° oven 25 to 30 minutes or until heated through.

Nutrition facts per serving: 534 cal., 32 g pro., 84 g carbo., 7 g total fat (1 g sat. fat), 43 mg chol., 2 g dietary fiber, 2,194 mg sodium. Daily Value: 41% vit. A, 73% vit. C, 43% iron.

Storage Hints

Because metal baking pans and aluminum foil can react with the acid in tomato products, keep these tips in mind when storing these dishes:

• Always use nonmetallic casseroles or baking dishes. Dishes with their own lids are best.

• To store tomato-based dishes in containers without lids, place a layer of plastic wrap over the food. Then, overwrap with foil.

• To heat the dish, remove foil and plastic wrap. Replace foil loosely over the container so foil does not touch the food.

ITALIAN CASSEROLE

MAKES 6 TO 8 SERVINGS
PREPARATION TIME: 30 MINUTES • CHILLING TIME: 8 HOURS
COOKING TIME: 45 MINUTES

½ pound bulk Italian sausage
½ pound ground raw turkey
1 large onion, chopped (1 cup)
1 teaspoon minced garlic (2 cloves)
1 15-ounce can Hunt's® Tomato Sauce
1 7½-ounce can Hunt's® Whole Tomatoes, cut up
1 6-ounce jar sliced mushrooms, drained
1 2¼-ounce can sliced pitted ripe olives, drained

¼ cup snipped fresh parsley
1 teaspoon dried basil, crushed
1 teaspoon dried oregano, crushed
¼ teaspoon pepper
6 ounces packaged dried wide noodles (3 cups), cooked and drained
¼ cup grated Parmesan cheese
1 cup shredded mozzarella cheese (4 ounces)

In Dutch oven cook sausage, turkey, onion, and garlic until meats are no longer are pink; drain. Stir in Hunt's Tomato Sauce, *undrained* Hunt's Whole Tomatoes (cut up), mushrooms, olives, parsley, basil, oregano, and pepper.

Bring to boiling; reduce heat. Simmer, uncovered, 5 minutes, stirring occasionally. Stir in noodles and Parmesan cheese.* Spread in greased 3-quart rectangular baking dish. Cover with plastic wrap, then foil. Refrigerate 8 to 24 hours.

To serve, remove plastic wrap. Stir once. Cover loosely with foil. Bake in 350° oven 40 minutes. Sprinkle with mozzarella. Bake, uncovered, 5 minutes more or until heated through.

*Note: To serve immediately, at this point, heat through. Transfer to serving dish. Sprinkle with mozzarella cheese.

Nutrition facts per serving: 370 cal., 23 g pro., 31 g carbo., 18 g total fat (7 g sat. fat), 74 mg chol., 3 g dietary fiber, 1,134 mg sodium. Daily Value: 15% vit. A, 36% vit. C, 24% iron.

GRILLED PORK SALAD

MAKES 4 SERVINGS
PREPARATION TIME: 25 MINUTES • MARINATING TIME: I HOUR
COOKING TIME: 12 MINUTES

4   **boneless pork loin chops, cut
    ¾ inch thick, or 4 medium
    skinless, boneless chicken breast
    halves (about I pound total)
Tomato Dressing (see recipe
    below)**

8   **cups torn mixed greens**
2   **cups favorite salad ingredients
    (such as cucumber, sweet
    pepper, celery, radish, carrot,
    and/or red cabbage, cut into
    bite-size pieces)**

Place pork in bowl. Pour about *1 cup* of the Tomato Dressing over; stir to coat evenly. Cover and refrigerate pork to marinate 1 to 2 hours.

To serve, remove pork, discarding marinade. Grill pork on uncovered grill directly over *medium-hot* coals (*medium* coals for chicken) 12 to 15 minutes or until tender and no longer pink, turning once.*

Arrange greens and desired salad ingredients on 4 individual plates. Thinly slice pork into bite-size strips; arrange on top of salads. Spoon some of the remaining Tomato Dressing over each salad.

Tomato Dressing: In bowl combine one 15-ounce can *Hunt's®* *Ready Tomato Sauces Chunky Special* and ¾ cup bottled *French salad dressing*. Store in tightly covered container in refrigerator up to 1 week.

*Note: If desired, place pork or chicken on unheated rack of broiler pan. Broil 4 to 5 inches from heat 12 to 15 minutes or until tender and no longer pink, turning once.

Nutrition facts per serving: 382 cal., 20 g pro., 23 g carbo., 24 g total fat (6 g sat. fat), 56 mg chol., 5 g dietary fiber, 960 mg sodium. Daily Value: 94% vit. A, 71% vit. C, 15% iron.

GREEK-STYLE BEEF AND POTATO BAKE

MAKES 4 SERVINGS
PREPARATION TIME: 30 MINUTES • CHILLING TIME: 8 HOURS
COOKING TIME: 40 MINUTES

1 pound ground beef or pork	⅛ teaspoon pepper
1 large onion, chopped (1 cup)	3 cups frozen loose-pack diced hash
1 teaspoon minced garlic (2 cloves)	brown potatoes with onion and
1 15-ounce can Hunt's® Ready	peppers
Tomato Sauces Original Italian	¾ cup crumbled feta cheese
¼ teaspoon salt	(3 ounces)
¼ teaspoon ground cinnamon	¼ cup grated Parmesan cheese

In skillet cook beef, onion, and garlic until meat is brown; drain. Stir in Hunt's Ready Tomato Sauces Original Italian, salt, cinnamon, and pepper. Bring to boiling; reduce heat. Simmer, covered, 10 minutes, stirring twice. Stir in frozen potatoes. Spoon into 2-quart square baking dish.* Cover with plastic wrap, then foil. Refrigerate 8 to 24 hours.

To serve, remove plastic wrap. Cover loosely with foil. Bake in 350° oven 30 minutes. Sprinkle with feta cheese and Parmesan cheese. Bake, uncovered, 10 minutes more or until potatoes are tender.

*__Note: To serve immediately,__ at this point, cover with foil and bake in 350° oven 20 minutes. Sprinkle with cheeses and continue with directions above.

Nutrition facts per serving: 483 cal., 33 g pro., 40 g carbo., 22 g total fat (10 g sat. fat), 96 mg chol., 6 g dietary fiber, 1,008 mg sodium. Daily Value: 24% vit. A, 53% vit. C, 31% iron.

Mix-and-Match Recipe

If your family would prefer a casserole with different seasonings, omit the cinnamon in the recipe above and replace the Hunt's® Ready Tomato Sauces Original Italian with Chunky Salsa or Chunky Special. Then, use cheddar or mozzarella cheese instead of feta cheese.

VINO ROSSO BRISKET

MAKES 12 SERVINGS
PREPARATION TIME: 30 MINUTES • CHILLING TIME: 8 HOURS
COOKING TIME: 2½ HOURS + 50 MINUTES

1 **3- to 4-pound fresh beef brisket**	3 **medium onions, chopped (1½ cups)**
¼ **teaspoon seasoned pepper**	1 **7½-ounce can Hunt's® Whole Tomatoes, cut up**
Dash salt	½ **cup port wine or beef broth**
1 **tablespoon all-purpose flour**	1 **envelope regular onion soup mix**
3 **medium carrots, chopped (1½ cups)**	2 **bay leaves**
3 **stalks celery, chopped (1½ cups)**	1 **teaspoon dried basil, crushed**

Sprinkle brisket with seasoned pepper and salt. Place flour in large oven cooking bag and shake; add brisket. Set bag in roasting pan.

In bowl combine carrots, celery, onions, *undrained* Hunt's Whole Tomatoes (cut up), wine, soup mix, bay leaves, and basil; pour over brisket. Close bag; cut slits in top.

Roast in 325° oven 2½ to 3 hours or until brisket is tender.* Cool slightly in bag; cover and refrigerate 8 to 24 hours.

To serve, remove meat and slice across grain into ¼-inch-thick slices. Place in 3-quart rectangular baking dish. Discard bay leaves. Skim fat from juices; pour over meat. Bake, covered, in 300° oven 50 minutes or until meat and juices are heated through. Spoon juices over meat.

Note: If desired, divide into 2 portions; serve 1 portion immediately. Wrap remaining portion in plastic wrap, then foil; label and freeze 1 to 3 months. Thaw in refrigerator before heating.

Nutrition facts per serving: 257 cal., 26 g pro., 10 g carbo., 11 g total fat (4 g sat. fat), 78 mg chol., 2 g dietary fiber, 416 mg sodium. Daily Value: 44% vit. A, 9% vit. C, 19% iron.

LASAGNA SPIRALS FLORENTINE

MAKES 6 SERVINGS
PREPARATION TIME: 30 MINUTES • CHILLING TIME: 8 HOURS
COOKING TIME: 65 MINUTES

1 pound ground beef	1 egg yolk
¼ cup finely chopped onion	¼ cup grated Parmesan cheese
1 15-ounce can Hunt's® Ready Tomato Sauces Original Italian	¼ cup milk
1 14½-ounce can Hunt's® Choice-Cut™ Diced Tomatoes with Italian Style Herbs	1 10-ounce package frozen chopped spinach, thawed and well drained
2 3-ounce packages cream cheese, softened	12 packaged dried lasagna noodles, cooked and drained
	1 cup shredded mozzarella cheese (4 ounces)

For sauce, in skillet cook beef and onion until meat is brown; drain. Stir in Hunt's Ready Tomato Sauces Original Italian and *undrained* Hunt's Choice-Cut Diced Tomatoes with Italian Style Herbs.

Bring to boiling; reduce heat. Simmer, uncovered, 5 minutes or until desired consistency. Spread about *half* of the sauce in 3-quart rectangular baking dish.

For filling, in bowl combine cream cheese, egg yolk, Parmesan cheese, and milk; stir in spinach. Spread about *2 tablespoons* filling over *each* noodle. Roll up, jelly-roll style; place rolls on top of sauce in dish. Spoon remaining sauce over top.* Cover with plastic wrap, then foil. Refrigerate 8 to 24 hours.

To serve, remove plastic wrap. Cover loosely with foil. Bake in 350° oven 1 hour. Sprinkle with mozzarella cheese. Bake, uncovered, 5 minutes more or until heated through.

***Note: To serve immediately,** at this point, cover loosely with foil and bake in 350° oven 40 minutes. Sprinkle with cheese. Bake, uncovered, 5 minutes or until heated through.

Nutrition facts per serving: 507 cal., 31 g pro., 43 g carbo., 24 g total fat (12 g sat. fat), 129 mg chol., 2 g dietary fiber, 936 mg sodium. Daily Value: 62% vit. A, 33% vit. C, 29% iron.

CROCKERY-COOKER POT ROAST

MAKES 8 SERVINGS
PREPARATION TIME: 15 MINUTES • COOKING TIME: 10 HOURS

1 2- to 2½-pound boneless beef chuck pot roast	1 tablespoon quick-cooking tapioca
1 tablespoon Wesson® Oil	1 15-ounce can Hunt's® Ready Tomato Sauces Chunky Tomato
2 medium carrots, sliced into ½-inch pieces	1 6-ounce can Hunt's® Tomato Paste
2 stalks celery, sliced (1 cup)	1 tablespoon brown sugar
1 medium onion, sliced	1 tablespoon Worcestershire sauce
1 teaspoon minced garlic (2 cloves)	¼ teaspoon pepper
	4 cups hot cooked noodles

If necessary, cut roast to fit into 3½- or 4-quart crockery cooker. In skillet cook roast on all sides in hot Wesson Oil until brown. Meanwhile, in crockery cooker place carrots, celery, onion, and garlic. Sprinkle tapioca over vegetables. Place roast on top.

In bowl combine *undrained* Hunt's Ready Tomato Sauces Chunky Tomato, Hunt's Tomato Paste, brown sugar, Worcestershire sauce, and pepper. Pour over roast.

Cover; cook on low-heat setting 10 to 12 hours. (Or, cook on high-heat setting 4 to 5 hours.) Transfer meat and vegetables to platter. Skim fat from tomato mixture; pass with meat and vegetables. Serve with noodles.

Nutrition facts per serving: 373 cal., 33 g pro., 34 g carbo., 11 g total fat (4 g sat. fat), 109 mg chol., 5 g dietary fiber, 513 mg sodium. Daily Value: 55% vit. A, 40% vit. C, 37% iron.

Check Your Crockery Cooker

This recipe is designed to be used with a 3½- or 4-quart crockery cooker with heating coils that wrap around the cooker. This type of cooker provides continuous slow cooking at one temperature. The timing will not work for a cooker with heating elements that sit below the cooking container and cycle on and off.

STUFFED CABBAGE ROLLS

MAKES 4 SERVINGS
PREPARATION TIME: 50 MINUTES • CHILLING TIME: 8 HOURS
COOKING TIME: 40 MINUTES

8 large cabbage leaves	$\frac{1}{3}$ cup long grain rice
$\frac{3}{4}$ pound ground pork	1 tablespoon Worcestershire sauce
1 small onion, chopped ($\frac{1}{3}$ cup)	$\frac{1}{4}$ teaspoon salt
1 8-ounce can Hunt's® Tomato Sauce	$\frac{1}{8}$ teaspoon pepper
$\frac{2}{3}$ cup water	1 15-ounce can Hunt's® Ready Tomato Sauces Chunky Special

Remove center veins from cabbage, keeping each leaf in one piece. Immerse leaves, *half* at a time, into boiling water 3 minutes or until limp; drain.

For filling, in skillet cook ground pork and onion until meat no longer is pink; drain. Stir in Hunt's Tomato Sauce, water, *uncooked* rice, Worcestershire sauce, salt, and pepper. Bring to boiling; reduce heat. Simmer, covered, 20 minutes. Let stand, covered, 5 minutes.

Place about $\frac{1}{3}$ *cup* meat mixture on *each* cabbage leaf; fold in sides. Starting at an unfolded edge, carefully roll up each leaf, making sure folded sides are included in roll. Place in 2-quart rectangular baking dish.* Cover and refrigerate 8 to 24 hours.

To serve, pour Hunt's Ready Tomato Sauces Chunky Special over cabbage rolls. Cover loosely with foil. Bake in 350° oven 40 to 45 minutes or until heated through.

***Note: To serve immediately,** at this point, pour Hunt's Ready Tomato Sauces Chunky Special over cabbage rolls. Cover loosely with foil. Bake in 350° oven 40 to 45 minutes or until heated through.

Nutrition facts per serving: 178 cal., 13 g pro., 16 g carbo., 6 g total fat (0 g sat. fat), 40 mg chol., 4 g dietary fiber, 1,251 mg sodium. Daily Value: 16% vit. A, 69% vit. C, 12% iron.

Black Bean Chili

Makes 8 Servings
Preparation Time: 25 Minutes • Freezing Time: Up to 3 Months
Cooking Time: 50 Minutes

4 large green sweet peppers, coarsely chopped (4 cups)
2 large onions, chopped (2 cups)
2 tablespoons Wesson® Oil
4 cups fresh or frozen whole kernel corn
2 to 4 teaspoons chili powder
2 15-ounce cans black beans, rinsed and drained
2 15-ounce cans Hunt's® Tomato Sauce
2 14½-ounce cans Hunt's® Choice-Cut™ Diced Tomatoes with Roasted Garlic
2 fresh, pickled, or canned jalapeño peppers, seeded and chopped* (optional)
½ teaspoon salt
½ teaspoon black pepper

In Dutch oven cook sweet peppers and onions in hot Wesson Oil over medium-high heat 2 minutes or until vegetables are crisp-tender. Remove from Dutch oven.

Add corn; cook and stir 2 minutes. (If necessary, add more oil.) Add chili powder; cook and stir 1 to 2 minutes more or until corn is crisp-tender.

Return pepper mixture to Dutch oven. Stir in black beans, Hunt's Tomato Sauce, *undrained* Hunt's Choice-Cut Diced Tomatoes with Roasted Garlic, jalapeño peppers (if desired), salt, and black pepper. Transfer *half* of the mixture to freezer container. Seal, label, and freeze up to 3 months. (Cook the remaining half of the mixture until heated through. Serve immediately.)

To serve frozen mixture, place in saucepan or Dutch oven with ¼ cup *water*. Cover and cook over medium-low heat 50 minutes or until heated through, stirring occasionally.

Note: Because jalapeño peppers contain oils that can burn skin and eyes, wear plastic or rubber gloves or work under cold running water when handling the peppers. If your bare hands touch the peppers, wash your hands and nails well with soap and water.

Nutrition facts per serving: 263 cal., 12 g pro., 51 g carbo., 5 g total fat (1 g sat. fat), 0 mg chol., 11 g dietary fiber, 1,510 mg sodium. Daily Value: 24% vit. A, 109% vit. C, 21% iron.

Rice- and Bean-Stuffed Peppers

Makes 4 Servings
Preparation Time: 25 Minutes • Freezing Time: Up to 1 Month
Cooking Time: 1 Hour

2 large sweet peppers (green, yellow, or red)
1 cup loose-pack frozen whole kernel corn
1 medium onion, chopped (½ cup)
1 15-ounce can Hunt's® Ready Tomato Sauces Chunky Chili

½ cup quick-cooking rice
1 15-ounce can red kidney beans, drained
¼ cup shredded mozzarella cheese (1 ounce)

Halve peppers lengthwise, removing stems, seeds, and membranes. Place in lightly greased 2- or 3-quart rectangular baking dish. Set aside.

In saucepan cook corn and onion, covered, in small amount of boiling water 4 to 5 minutes or until tender; drain and set aside. Reserve ⅓ *cup* of the Hunt's Ready Tomato Sauces Chunky Chili; set aside.

In same saucepan combine remaining tomato sauce, *uncooked* rice, and ⅓ cup *water*. Bring to boiling; remove from heat. Cover; let stand 5 minutes. Stir in beans and corn mixture. Spoon into peppers, filling just even with top edges. Spoon any remaining mixture around peppers. Spoon reserved sauce over peppers.* Cover with plastic wrap, then foil. Label and freeze up to 1 month. (Or, cover and refrigerate 8 to 24 hours.)

To serve, remove plastic wrap. Cover loosely with foil. Bake frozen peppers in 375° oven 1 hour or until heated through. (Or, bake refrigerated peppers 40 to 45 minutes.) Sprinkle with mozzarella cheese.

*__Note: To serve immediately,__ at this point, cover loosely with foil. Bake in 375° oven 15 minutes or until heated through. Sprinkle with mozzarella cheese.

Nutrition facts per serving: 231 cal., 12 g pro., 47 g carbo., 2 g total fat (1 g sat. fat), 4 mg chol., 8 g dietary fiber, 751 mg sodium. Daily Value: 20% vit. A, 56% vit. C, 17% iron.

SATISFYING SOUPS, CHILIES, AND STEWS

Your family will love this creative collection of meals in a bowl, great for serving year-round. Thanks to Hunt's® tomato products, these recipes go beyond the typical thin-broth soup to offer hearty, satisfying flavors in concoctions such as Bean and Squash Soup, Italian Chili, and Seafood Gumbo.

Bean and Squash Soup
(see recipe, page 82)

BEAN AND SQUASH SOUP

MAKES 4 SERVINGS
PREPARATION TIME: 20 MINUTES • COOKING TIME: 15 MINUTES

2½ cups water
1 cup chopped, peeled, and seeded
   butternut squash or sliced
   carrots
1 15-ounce can Hunt's® Ready
   Tomato Sauces Chunky Special
1 15-ounce can black beans or red
   kidney beans, rinsed and drained
1 cup frozen or drained canned
   baby corn, cut crosswise into
   ½-inch-long pieces, or frozen
   whole kernel corn

1 small onion, quartered lengthwise
   and sliced
2 teaspoons instant beef bouillon
   granules or 2 vegetable bouillon
   cubes
1¼ teaspoons chili powder
1 teaspoon dried oregano, crushed
½ teaspoon minced garlic (1 clove)
¼ teaspoon ground cumin
   Dairy sour cream (optional)
   Snipped fresh parsley (optional)

In saucepan combine water and squash. Bring to boiling; reduce heat. Simmer, covered, 5 minutes.

Stir in Hunt's Ready Tomato Sauces Chunky Special, beans, corn, onion, bouillon granules, chili powder, oregano, garlic, and cumin. Return to boiling; reduce heat. Simmer, covered, 10 to 15 minutes more or until squash is tender. If desired, garnish with sour cream and parsley.

Nutrition facts per serving: 193 cal., 10 g pro., 41 g carbo., 3 g total fat (0 g sat. fat), 0 mg chol., 8 g dietary fiber, 1,175 mg sodium. Daily Value: 44% vit. A, 39% vit. C, 13% iron.

Topping Off a Soup or Stew

Add the perfect finishing touch to a steaming bowl of soup or stew by sprinkling it with Orville Redenbacher's® Gourmet® Popping Corn. Choose Original or White Popping Corn and pop it in your hot-air popper for a simple, yet crunchy, topping. Or, select a favorite flavor of Microwave Popping Corn to enjoy as a quick and tasty soup accent.

TURKEY AND BLACK BEAN SOUP

MAKES 4 OR 5 SERVINGS
PREPARATION TIME: 10 MINUTES • COOKING TIME: 12 MINUTES

2 14½-ounce cans chicken broth
1 15-ounce can black beans, rinsed
   and drained
1 14½-ounce can Hunt's® Choice-
   Cut™ Diced Tomatoes with
   Roasted Garlic

1 cup loose-pack frozen whole
   kernel corn
1 teaspoon dried oregano, crushed
¼ teaspoon ground cumin
6 ounces fully cooked smoked
   turkey sausage, halved
   lengthwise and thinly sliced

In saucepan combine broth, beans, *undrained* Hunt's Choice-Cut Diced Tomatoes with Roasted Garlic, corn, oregano, and cumin. Bring to boiling; reduce heat. Simmer, uncovered, 3 minutes. Stir in sausage; heat through.

Nutrition facts per serving: 220 cal., 21 g pro., 30 g carbo., 5 g total fat (1 g sat. fat), 28 mg chol., 6 g dietary fiber, 1,705 mg sodium. Daily Value: 8% vit. A, 26% vit. C, 17% iron.

PRONTO TURKEY-VEGETABLE SOUP

MAKES 6 SERVINGS
PREPARATION TIME: 15 MINUTES • COOKING TIME: 15 MINUTES

1½ pounds ground raw turkey or
    chicken
¼   cup finely chopped onion
½   teaspoon chili powder
1   27½-ounce can Hunt's® Original
    Spaghetti Sauce with
    Mushrooms

2 cups chicken broth
1 16-ounce package frozen mixed
   vegetables
½ cup shredded Healthy Choice®
   Cheddar Cheese (2 ounces)

In saucepan cook ground turkey and onion until meat no longer is pink; drain. Stir in chili powder; cook and stir 1 minute. Stir in Hunt's Original Spaghetti Sauce with Mushrooms, chicken broth, and frozen vegetables.

Bring to boiling; reduce heat. Simmer, covered, 10 minutes or until vegetables are tender. Sprinkle servings with Healthy Choice Cheddar Cheese.

Nutrition facts per serving: 317 cal., 25 g pro., 30 g carbo., 13 g total fat (2 g sat. fat), 44 mg chol., 7 g dietary fiber, 1,450 mg sodium. Daily Value: 47% vit. A, 38% vit. C, 26% iron.

Chicken-Cannellini Stew

MAKES 4 OR 5 SERVINGS
PREPARATION TIME: 10 MINUTES • COOKING TIME: 12 MINUTES

1 large onion, chopped (1 cup)	1 14½-ounce can Hunt's® Choice-Cut™ Diced Tomatoes with Roasted Garlic
1 tablespoon Wesson® Oil	
1 19-ounce can white kidney (cannellini) beans	1 cup loose-pack frozen peas
1 15-ounce can Hunt's® Ready Tomato Sauces Chunky Chili	2 cups cubed cooked chicken
	4 ounces cheddar or Monterey Jack cheese, cut into shavings or shredded (optional)

In saucepan cook onion in hot Wesson Oil until tender. Stir in *undrained* beans, Hunt's Ready Tomato Sauces Chunky Chili, *undrained* Hunt's Choice-Cut Diced Tomatoes with Roasted Garlic, and peas.

Bring to boiling; reduce heat. Simmer, covered, 5 minutes. Stir in chicken; heat through. If desired, top each serving with cheese.

Nutrition facts per serving: 446 cal., 35 g pro., 49 g carbo., 12 g total fat (3 g sat. fat), 58 mg chol., 4 g dietary fiber, 1,070 mg sodium. Daily Value: 29% vit. A, 43% vit. C, 29% iron.

Timesaving Ingredients

Speed up meal preparation by relying on some of these work-freeing and timesaving ingredients you can find in the supermarket.

• In the grocery aisle, choose Hunt's® Ready Tomato Sauces or Hunt's® Spaghetti Sauces.

• In the freezer case, look for frozen chopped cooked chicken, frozen chopped onion or sweet pepper, and frozen hash brown potatoes.

• In the produce department, you'll find bottled minced garlic, packaged coleslaw mix, packaged salad mixtures, and precut vegetable dippers.

• In the refrigerator/deli section, select shredded cheeses or sliced meats.

PORK RAGOUT WITH BABY CARROTS

MAKES 6 SERVINGS
PREPARATION TIME: 20 MINUTES • COOKING TIME: 1 HOUR

1½ pounds pork stew meat, cut into
    1-inch pieces
  2 tablespoons Wesson® Oil
  1 medium onion, thinly sliced
  1 tablespoon finely chopped
    gingerroot or ½ teaspoon
    ground ginger
  1 teaspoon minced garlic (2 cloves)

  1 14½-ounce can Hunt's® Choice-
    Cut™ Diced Tomatoes
1¼ cups chicken broth
  ½ teaspoon salt
  ¼ teaspoon pepper
  ½ pound baby-cut carrots, peeled
  2 tablespoons all-purpose flour
    Hot cooked noodles, couscous, or
    rice (optional)

In Dutch oven cook meat, *half* at a time, in hot Wesson Oil over medium-high heat until brown, adding onion, gingerroot, and garlic with second portion of meat; drain. Return all meat to Dutch oven.

Stir in *undrained* Hunt's Choice-Cut Diced Tomatoes, *1 cup* of the broth, the salt, and pepper. Bring to boiling; reduce heat. Simmer, covered, 30 minutes. Add carrots. Return to boiling; reduce heat. Simmer, covered, 20 minutes more or until meat and carrots are tender.

In screw-top jar shake remaining broth and flour; add to Dutch oven. Cook and stir until thickened and bubbly. Cook and stir 1 minute more. If desired, serve over noodles.

Nutrition facts per serving: 293 cal., 17 g pro., 12 g carbo., 20 g total fat (7 g sat. fat), 60 mg chol., 3 g dietary fiber, 716 mg sodium. Daily Value: 90% vit. A, 21% vit. C, 12% iron.

CURRIED PORK STEW

MAKES 4 SERVINGS
PREPARATION TIME: 30 MINUTES • COOKING TIME: 1 HOUR

¾ pound lean boneless pork, cut into
    ¾-inch pieces
1 medium onion, chopped (½ cup)
1 teaspoon minced garlic (2 cloves)
1 tablespoon Wesson® Oil
2 to 3 teaspoons curry powder
¼ teaspoon ground ginger
    Dash to ⅛ teaspoon ground red
    pepper

¼ cup water
1 tablespoon all-purpose flour
1 14½-ounce can Hunt's® Choice-
    Cut™ Diced Tomatoes
2 medium carrots, sliced (1 cup)
1 sweet potato, peeled and cut into
    bite-size pieces
¼ cup mixed dried fruit bits
¼ cup chopped peanuts

In skillet cook meat, onion, and garlic in hot Wesson Oil over medium-high heat until meat is brown. Stir in curry powder, ginger, and red pepper. Cook and stir 1 minute.

In 2-quart round casserole stir together water and flour. Stir in *undrained* Hunt's Choice-Cut Diced Tomatoes, carrots, potato, and fruit bits. Stir in meat mixture.

Bake, covered, in 350° oven 1 hour or until meat is tender. Sprinkle servings with peanuts.

Nutrition facts per serving: 295 cal., 17 g pro., 28 g carbo., 14 g total fat (3 g sat. fat), 38 mg chol., 4 g dietary fiber, 520 mg sodium. Daily Value: 168% vit. A, 50% vit. C, 12% iron.

Gingerroot on Call

Fresh gingerroot adds a delightful accent to many dishes, such as the stew above. It's easy to keep some on hand. Just peel the gingerroot and slice it. Then cover the slices with Wesson® Oil and refrigerate in a covered container for up to 3 months. Or, freeze the root in a freezer bag, and grate what you need from the frozen root.

ITALIAN CHILI

MAKES 6 TO 8 SERVINGS
PREPARATION TIME: 20 MINUTES • COOKING TIME: 20 MINUTES

½ pound bulk Italian sausage*
½ pound ground beef
1 large onion, chopped (1 cup)
1 small green sweet pepper, chopped (½ cup)
2 14½-ounce cans Hunt's® Choice-Cut™ Diced Tomatoes with Roasted Garlic
1 15-ounce can small white beans, drained
1 teaspoon sugar

1 teaspoon dried Italian seasoning, crushed
1 teaspoon instant beef bouillon granules
¼ to ½ teaspoon salt
⅛ teaspoon crushed red pepper (optional)
½ cup shredded mozzarella cheese (2 ounces) or ¼ cup grated Parmesan cheese (optional)

In Dutch oven cook sausage, ground beef, onion, and sweet pepper until meat no longer is pink; drain.

Stir in *undrained* Hunt's Choice-Cut Diced Tomatoes with Roasted Garlic, beans, sugar, Italian seasoning, bouillon granules, salt, and, if desired, red pepper.

Bring to boiling; reduce heat. Simmer, covered, 15 to 20 minutes. If desired, top servings with mozzarella cheese.

Note: If you like mild chili, choose bulk sweet Italian sausage. For chili with just a little hotness, use bulk hot Italian sausage. To make this chili extra spicy, substitute 1 pound bulk hot Italian sausage for the ½ pound sausage and the ½ pound ground beef.

Nutrition facts per serving: 294 cal., 20 g pro., 26 g carbo., 12 g total fat (4 g sat. fat), 45 mg chol., 1 g dietary fiber, 1,422 mg sodium. Daily Value: 10% vit. A, 47% vit. C, 18% iron.

SAVORY SAUSAGE RAGOUT

MAKES 4 SERVINGS
PREPARATION TIME: 20 MINUTES • COOKING TIME: 25 MINUTES

1 pound fresh Italian sausage links, cut into ½-inch-thick slices	1 cup sliced fresh mushrooms
1 large onion, chopped (1 cup)	2 tablespoons snipped fresh parsley
1 large green sweet pepper, chopped (1 cup)	2 small zucchini, sliced, or one 14-ounce can artichoke hearts, drained and quartered
1 14½-ounce can Hunt's® Choice-Cut™ Diced Tomatoes with Italian Style Herbs	½ pound packaged dried cavatelli or mostaccioli, cooked and drained
1 8-ounce can Hunt's® Tomato Sauce	¼ cup grated Parmesan cheese

In Dutch oven cook sausage over medium heat until brown; drain, reserving 2 tablespoons drippings in pan. Drain sausage on paper towels; set aside.

Cook onion and sweet pepper in reserved drippings until tender; drain. Stir in *undrained* Hunt's Choice-Cut Diced Tomatoes with Italian Style Herbs, Hunt's Tomato Sauce, mushrooms, parsley, and sausage.

Bring to boiling; reduce heat. Simmer, covered, 10 minutes, stirring occasionally. Stir in zucchini. Return to boiling; reduce heat. Simmer, uncovered, 5 minutes more or until zucchini is tender. Serve over cavatelli. Sprinkle with Parmesan cheese.

Nutrition facts per serving: 677 cal., 27 g pro., 61 g carbo., 37 g total fat (12 g sat. fat), 94 mg chol., 4 g dietary fiber, 2,033 mg sodium. Daily Value: 17% vit. A, 90% vit. C, 35% iron.

Seafood Gumbo

Makes 8 Servings
Preparation Time: 30 Minutes • Cooking Time: 40 Minutes

1 pound fresh or frozen skinless
    cod, orange roughy, haddock, or
    catfish fillets, ½ to ¾ inch thick
½ pound fresh or frozen peeled and
    deveined shrimp
½ cup all-purpose flour
½ cup Wesson® Oil
2 large green sweet peppers,
    chopped (2 cups)
3½ cups chicken broth

2 14½-ounce cans Hunt's® Choice-
    Cut™ Diced Tomatoes with
    Roasted Garlic
¼ to ½ teaspoon ground red pepper
1 10-ounce package frozen cut okra,
    thawed
1 8-ounce package crab-flavored
    chunk-style fish
4 cups hot cooked rice

Thaw fish and shrimp, if frozen. Cut fish into 1-inch pieces. Cover and refrigerate fish and shrimp until needed.

In heavy Dutch oven stir together flour and Wesson Oil until smooth. Cook over medium-high heat 5 minutes, stirring constantly with wooden spoon. Reduce heat to medium. Cook and stir 10 minutes more or until a reddish brown roux forms. Add sweet peppers. Continue cooking and stirring over medium heat 5 to 10 minutes or until very tender.

Carefully stir in chicken broth, *undrained* Hunt's Choice-Cut Diced Tomatoes with Roasted Garlic, and red pepper. Bring to boiling; reduce heat. Simmer, covered, 20 minutes.

Add thawed okra. Return to boiling; reduce heat. Simmer, uncovered, 7 minutes. Add fish, shrimp, and crab-flavored fish. Return just to boiling; reduce heat. Simmer, covered, 2 to 5 minutes or until shrimp turn pink and fish flakes easily with a fork. Serve over rice.

Nutrition facts per serving: 410 cal., 24 g pro., 43 g carbo., 16 g total fat (2 g sat. fat), 71 mg chol., 2 g dietary fiber, 1,091 mg sodium. Daily Value: 17% vit. A, 148% vit. C, 20% iron.

Fish Stew Provençal

MAKES 8 SERVINGS
PREPARATION TIME: 25 MINUTES • COOKING TIME: 25 MINUTES

1½ pounds fresh or frozen skinless whitefish fillets
2 cups sliced fresh mushrooms
1 large onion, chopped (1 cup)
1 large green sweet pepper, chopped (1 cup)
2 stalks celery, thinly sliced (1 cup)
1 teaspoon minced garlic (2 cloves)
1 tablespoon Wesson® Oil
1 28-ounce can Hunt's® Crushed Tomatoes
1 8-ounce can Hunt's® Tomato Sauce
½ teaspoon dried thyme, crushed
½ teaspoon dried oregano, crushed
¼ teaspoon dried basil, crushed
¼ teaspoon black pepper
Hot cooked orzo or rice (optional)

Thaw fish, if frozen. Cut into 1-inch pieces. Set aside. In Dutch oven cook mushrooms, onion, sweet pepper, celery, and garlic in hot Wesson Oil over medium-high heat 5 minutes or until tender. Stir in *undrained* Hunt's Crushed Tomatoes, Hunt's Tomato Sauce, thyme, oregano, basil, and black pepper.

Bring to boiling; reduce heat. Simmer, covered, 15 minutes. Stir in fish. Cook, covered, 5 minutes more or until fish flakes easily with a fork. If desired, serve over orzo.

Nutrition facts per serving: 135 cal., 16 g pro., 13 g carbo., 3 g total fat (0 g sat. fat), 32 mg chol., 3 g dietary fiber, 506 mg sodium. Daily Value: 11% vit. A, 44% vit. C, 11% iron.

Fish Alternatives

Whitefish is a firm-textured fish that adds a delicate flavor to stews like the one above. If you can't find whitefish at your fish market or supermarket, substitute haddock, halibut, orange roughy, red snapper, or sole.

RECIPE INDEX

Recipe Index (continued)

RECIPES-BY-PRODUCT INDEX

RECIPES-BY-PRODUCT INDEX (CONTINUED)

NUTRITION FIGURES

Each recipe in this book lists the nutrition facts for one serving. Here's how these values were calculated. When a recipe gives a choice of ingredients (such as ground beef or pork), the first choice was used for the analysis. If an ingredient is listed as optional in a recipe, it was not included in the analysis. All values were rounded to the nearest whole number.